1st EDITION

Perspectives on Diseases and Disorders

Deafness and Hearing Impairment

Clay Farris Naff
Book Editor

GALE
CENGAGE Learning™

Detroit • New York • San Francisco • New Haven, Conn • Waterville, Maine • London

KH

GALE
CENGAGE Learning™

Christine Nasso, *Publisher*
Elizabeth Des Chenes, *Managing Editor*

© 2010 Greenhaven Press, a part of Gale, Cengage Learning

Articles in Greenhaven Press anthologies are often edited for length to meet page requirements. In addition, original titles of these works are changed to clearly present the main thesis and to explicitly indicate the author's opinion. Every effort is made to ensure that Greenhaven Press accurately reflects the original intent of the authors. Every effort has been made to trace the owners of copyrighted material.

Cover image copyright © Gabe Palmer/Surf/Corbis.

LIBRARY OF CONGRESS CATALOGING-IN-PUBLICATION DATA

Deafness and hearing impairment / Clay Farris Naff, book editor.
   p. cm. -- (Perspectives on diseases and disorders)
Includes bibliographical references and index.
ISBN 978-0-7377-4788-1 (hardcover)
1. Deafness--Popular works. 2. Hearing impaired--Popular works. I. Naff, Clay Farris.
RF290.D426 2010
617.8--dc22

            2009048652

Printed in the United States of America
1 2 3 4 5 6 7 14 13 12 11 10

8/17/11

CONTENTS

CHAPTER 1   Understanding Deafness and Hearing Impairment

FOREWORD

"Medicine, to produce health, has to examine disease."
—Plutarch

Independent research on a health issue is often the first step to complement discussions with a physician. But locating accurate, well-organized, understandable medical information can be a challenge. A simple Internet search on terms such as "cancer" or "diabetes," for example, returns an intimidating number of results. Sifting through the results can be daunting, particularly when some of the information is inconsistent or even contradictory. The Greenhaven Press series Perspectives on Diseases and Disorders offers a solution to the often overwhelming nature of researching diseases and disorders.

From the clinical to the personal, titles in the Perspectives on Diseases and Disorders series provide students and other researchers with authoritative, accessible information in unique anthologies that include basic information about the disease or disorder, controversial aspects of diagnosis and treatment, and first-person accounts of those impacted by the disease. The result is a well-rounded combination of primary and secondary sources that, together, provide the reader with a better understanding of the disease or disorder.

Each volume in Perspectives on Diseases and Disorders explores a particular disease or disorder in detail. Material for each volume is carefully selected from a wide range of sources, including encyclopedias, journals, newspapers, nonfiction books, speeches, government documents, pamphlets, organization newsletters, and position papers. Articles in the first chapter provide an authoritative, up-to-date overview that covers symptoms, causes and effects, treatments, cures, and medical advances. The second chapter presents a substantial number of opposing viewpoints on controversial treatments and other current debates relating to the volume topic. The third chapter offers a variety of personal perspectives on the disease or disorder. Patients, doctors, caregivers, and loved ones represent just some of the voices found in this narrative chapter.

Each Perspectives on Diseases and Disorders volume also includes:

- An **annotated table of contents** that provides a brief summary of each article in the volume.
- An **introduction** specific to the volume topic.
- Full-color **charts and graphs** to illustrate key points, concepts, and theories.
- Full-color **photos** that show aspects of the disease or disorder and enhance textual material.
- **"Fast Facts"** that highlight pertinent additional statistics and surprising points.
- A **glossary** providing users with definitions of important terms.
- A **chronology** of important dates relating to the disease or disorder.
- An annotated list of **organizations to contact** for students and other readers seeking additional information.
- A **bibliography** of additional books and periodicals for further research.
- A detailed **subject index** that allows readers to quickly find the information they need.

Whether a student researching a disorder, a patient recently diagnosed with a disease, or an individual who simply wants to learn more about a particular disease or disorder, a reader who turns to Perspectives on Diseases and Disorders will find a wealth of information in each volume that offers not only basic information, but also vigorous debate from multiple perspectives.

INTRODUCTION

Consider which of your senses you value most. When asked this in an online poll, some people answered "common sense," but most named sight as the one sense they would most hate to lose. The loss of any sense is undoubtedly life-changing, but a strong case can be made that nothing contributes more to human interaction than the sense of hearing.

People are social animals, and above all else spoken language is what connects individuals to one another. Without the ability to hear, deaf people are largely isolated from the mainstream of society. To communicate they have had to invent an alternative to oral language. They have done this with great ingenuity, only to be met with suspicion, ridicule, and discouragement. The hearing impaired also face obstacles to social acceptance. They are often marginalized.

This marginalization is evidenced by the simple fact that famous deaf people do not easily come to mind—at least not outside the Deaf community.

There are exceptions, of course. Composer Ludwig van Beethoven lost his hearing before completing his famous Ninth Symphony. Baseball player William Ellsworth Hoy hit the first grand slam in the American League. He is also credited with inventing the hand signals that umpires use even today for strikes and outs. Actress Marlee Matlin achieved great fame when she won the Academy Award for Best Actress for her debut performance in the 1986 film *Children of a Lesser God*. However, even she feels that she has been pigeonholed by her disability. Noting that she has been in show business for decades, having won the Oscar at the age of twenty-one

Deaf baseball player William Ellsworth Hoy hit the first grand slam in the American League and is credited with inventing umpire hand signals in use to this day. (**Mark Rucker/ Transcendental Graphics, Getty Images**)

and having subsequently starred in both films and television series, Matlin remarked in a 2004 interview, "At some point we have to stop and say 'there's Marlee' not 'there's the deaf actress.'"[1]

Yet, the fact remains that deaf and hearing-impaired people, though certainly hardworking and capable of achievement, tend to be marginalized. Deafness and hearing impairment make communication with hearing people difficult, and that seems to trigger prejudice on the part of the hearing. The late deaf educator Leo M. Jacobs reflected on this in an essay written shortly before his death in 1998:

Deafness and the communication disability associated with it have placed deaf people in a minority group within a majority of people who hear and speak. The disability has given us our own language, which has spawned a separate community and culture. We have survived and enjoyed full lives within our own society. . . . However, because we do have problems communicating with hearing people, there is a long history of prejudice and discrimination against us by the hearing majority.[2]

That prejudice is expressed in the contemporary use of the word "dumb." Historically, it appeared in the phrase "deaf and dumb," meaning unable to hear or speak. However, the disability was widely—and wrongly—assumed to mean that the person lacked the intellectual capacity for speech or learning. Hence, the word "dumb" came to mean "stupid." Cruel as this was, the prejudice against the deaf played out in an even crueler way. As deaf people developed sign language, they found that mainstream educators and even their parents discouraged them.

It seems highly probable that the deaf have always signed with one another, at least in an informal way. Starting in Europe in the 1500s, sign language began to be organized as a formal communication system. Within a century the first manual alphabet was published. However, sign language was met with widespread suspicion and contempt. In some countries, such as Germany, sign language was legally banned.

In the United States, the Reverend Thomas Hopkins Gallaudet took an interest in sign language after an encounter with a young deaf girl. On a trip to Europe he learned about the efforts of a French cleric to develop sign language—despite the staunch opposition of his own church hierarchy. He also met a remarkable deaf Frenchman named Laurent Clerc and persuaded him to accompany him to America.

Together they planted the seeds of deaf education by establishing the Hartford Asylum for the Education and Instruction of the Deaf and Dumb on April 15, 1817. Their efforts led to a rapid spread of what would soon become American Sign Language (ASL) among deaf people throughout America. In 1864 Gallaudet's son, along with Clerc and others, established the Columbia Institute for the Deaf in Washington, D.C. (since renamed Gallaudet University). However, at just about the same time, a movement opposing sign language arose. Led by inventor Alexander Graham Bell among others, it held that teaching lipreading and speech was paramount in the education of the deaf. Despite strong resistance from many deaf educators, this became the mainstream view for many decades to come. As a result, deaf people continued to be marginalized, since only in rare instances could they read lips and speak with the same facility as a hearing person. The use of sign language was widely condemned. Even Congress got into the act with an 1880 declaration touting "the incontestable superiority of speech over sign for integrating the deaf-mute into society and for giving him better command of the language."[3] Such attitudes guaranteed the deaf would remain in a second-class status—at best.

Throughout much of the twentieth century "oralism," as this method came to be known, dominated the education of the deaf at the expense of sign language. Frances Hunter, who grew up deaf in Shreveport, Louisiana, in the 1950s and 1960s, recalls how strongly her family and community wanted her to learn to speak. They insisted she attend an oral school, until she was thrown out. Only then was she sent to the Louisiana School for the Deaf in Baton Rouge to learn ASL. Hunter's family considered her a failure. "My parents didn't want me signing," Hunter told the *Shreveport Times*. "They thought signing was very gross."[4]

Fortunately, attitudes have changed. Oralism is out. The Deaf community has a stronger sense of identity than ever. Civil rights legislation has opened new doors

Edward Miner Gallaudet with his family. In 1864 he headed the Columbia Institute for the Deaf, now known as Gallaudet University. (© Bettman/Corbis)

and created remedies for those who have suffered unjust discrimination. Seemingly small things, like closed captioning on nearly all television shows, have improved the quality of life for the deaf and hearing impaired. Technological leaps, like the cochlear implant, have made it possible for some deaf people to hear for the first time.

Yet, as it so often does, progress has given rise to new controversies and discontent. Technological innovations have undermined the teaching of sign language to some extent. Parents can now choose to have a deaf child receive cochlear implants during infancy. This does not sit well with some Deaf advocates. In 2006 Gallaudet University erupted in protests over the selection of a new president whom some saw as not being sufficiently supportive of ASL and Deaf culture. At the same time, others, both hearing and deaf, have decried what they see as a misguided separatist movement.

In reality, however, deaf and hearing-impaired people, whether they choose to embrace technology or not, still have to find their way in a society where hearing predominates. "The truth is we cannot separate ourselves from hearing society at all," writes Mark Drolsbaugh, who runs a Web site called Deaf Culture Online. "The hearing world is everywhere. We couldn't escape from it even if we wanted to."[5] That being so, the growing range of choices for the deaf and hearing impaired may make it easier to feel at home in the world of the hearing.

Notes

1. Quoted in Dominick A. Miserandino, "Matlin, Marlee—Actress/Author/Producer," The Celebrity Cafe.com, August 2004. http://thecelebritycafe.com/interviews/marlee_matlin_2004_08.html.
2. Leo M. Jacobs, "Unconscious Discrimination," in Carol Erting, Robert C. Johnson, and Dorothy L. Smith, eds., *The Deaf Way*. Washington, DC: Gallaudet University Press, 1994, p. 684.
3. Quoted in Gabriel Grayson, *Talking with Your Hands, Listening with Your Eyes*. Garden City Park, NY: Square One, 2003, p. 5.
4. *Shreveport Times,* "Cultural Divide Exists Between Hearing and Deaf," January 24, 2009. www.4hearing loss.com/archives/2009/02/cultural_divide.html.
5. Mark Drolsbaugh, "The Isolation Myth," Deaf Culture Online, 2008. www.deaf-culture-online.com/isolation myth.html.

Understanding Deafness and Hearing Impairment

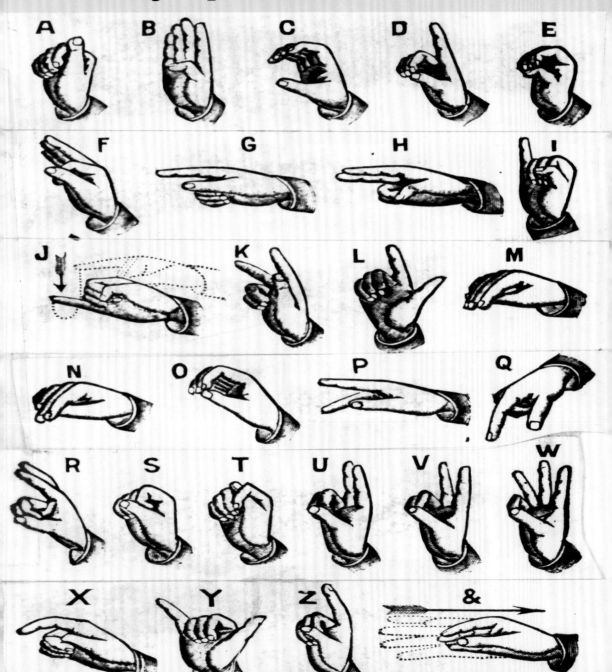

An Overview of Hearing Disorders

Brian Douglas Hoyle

In the following article researcher Brian Douglas Hoyle describes the wide range of disabilities that fall under the heading of hearing disorder. At one end of the spectrum, he indicates, is the inability to discriminate sounds that fall in a certain frequency range. At the other end is complete deafness. Many causes and symptoms fall within this spectrum. Some are congenital (that is, present at birth), and others are age-related. Both genetic and environmental factors are involved in hearing loss. Some people are born with a double set of genes that give rise to hearing loss. Others lose hearing to disease or damage from extreme noise. Even food sensitivities can cause hearing disorders, Hoyle says. A variety of treatments are available to cope with hearing loss. They range from simple ear-cleaning to surgery, he states. Hoyle holds a doctorate in microbiology. He lives in Nova Scotia, Canada.

Photo on previous page. Since it was first developed in 1817 by the Hartford Asylum, the Deaf and Dumb Alphabet has been helping the deaf communicate with each other and the speaking world. (© Bettmann/Corbis)

SOURCE: Brian Douglas Hoyle, *Gale Encyclopedia of Neurological Disorders,* Detroit, MI: Thomson Gale, 2005. Copyright © 2005 Thomson Gale, a part of The Thomson Corporation. Reproduced by permission of Gale, a part of Cengage Learning.

Hearing disorders range from a temporary, partial loss of hearing to the permanent loss of hearing known as deafness.

The variety of hearing disorders includes a loss or decrease in the ability to discern certain frequencies of sound, a ringing or other noise that is unrelated to any actual external sound, damage due to physical trauma or infection, and genetically determined structural malformation.

A Worldwide Affliction

Hearing disorders occur worldwide in all races. The hearing loss that occurs with age is very common, affecting an estimated 30% of Americans over 60 years of age and 50% of those older than 75.

Tinnitus, a ringing or noisy sensation in the ears, is quite common with an estimated 20% of people affected worldwide. In the United States alone, some 36 million people experience tinnitus.

For hearing loss caused by otosclerosis, middle-aged Caucasian women are more prone than others, perhaps as a consequence of hormonal changes. In otosclerosis, abnormal bone development occurs in the middle ear, resulting in progressive hearing loss. Sudden hearing loss happens more often to people ages 30–60 for unknown reasons.

Varieties of Hearing Loss

Presbycusis

Presbycusis (or sensorineural hearing loss) is the loss of hearing that occurs with age. The condition results from the long-term assault on the ear structures, particularly on the inner ear, from a lifetime of noise, ear infections, or growths on bones of the outer or middle ear. The inner ear is where the vibrational sound waves are converted to electrical signals, courtesy of thousands of tiny hairs that are in a fluid-enclosed space called the cochlea. The hairs are connected to nerve cells, which send the electrical signals to the brain.

Most age-related hearing loss is due to damage to the cochlea. The tiny hairs can bend or even break, and the attached nerve cells can degenerate. The resulting less-efficient transmission of the electrical signal, particularly of higher-pitched tones, causes hearing loss.

Symptoms of presbycusis typically include increased difficulty in making out sounds of a certain volume or tone, especially when background sounds are present.

Conductive hearing loss

In conductive hearing loss, sound is not transmitted efficiently through the outer and middle ears. These regions house the eardrum, ear canal, and the trio of tiny bones (ossicles) in the middle ear that transmits sound energy to the inner ear. The hearing loss can be due to malformation of structures like the canal or the ossicles, dense buildup of ear wax, or fluid in the ear due to colds, allergies, or infections like otitis media. Symptoms include a decreased ability to detect fainter sounds and a general lowering of the sound level that can be detected.

Otitis media

Otitis media is an inflammation in the middle ear that is usually accompanied by fluid buildup. The condition may be transient in some children, but persistent in others to the point of requiring surgical correction. In developed countries, otitis media is second to the common cold as the most common health problem in preschool-aged children. Hearing loss occurs because of the fluid accumulation and the resulting suppression of sound waves moving to the inner ear.

Central auditory processing disorders

Central auditory processing disorders result in hearing loss when the areas of the brain involved in hearing are dam-

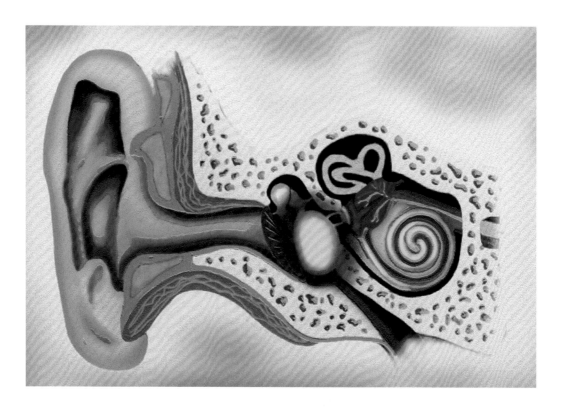

aged. Sources of damage include disease, injury, and tumor growth. Consistent with the variety of causes, the symptoms of the disorders include the inability to hear certain sounds, inability to tell one sound from another, and the inability to recognize a pattern such as speech in sounds.

Otitis media is a type of hearing disorder that affects the middle ear and is accompanied by pus buildup and sometimes requires corrective surgery. (VEM/Photo Researchers, Inc.)

Congenital hearing loss

Congenital hearing loss is present from birth and is caused by a genetic defect or disturbance during fetal development. Genetic factors cause more than half of all such disorders. Depending on the nature of the genetic defect, the occurrence of the hearing loss may be common or rare. For example, if both parents have a genetically determined hearing deficiency, the chance of passing the trait to their children is high. In other cases, people who have normal hearing carry a second, defective copy of a crucial gene. The chance of passing on the hearing loss is 25%.

Hearing loss at birth can also be caused by pre-birth infections such as measles, cytomegalovirus, or herpes simplex virus.

Otosclerosis

The abnormal growth of the bone of the middle ear prevents the ossicles, particularly the last of the trio of bones (the stapes), from properly transmitting sound waves to the inner ear in otosclerosis. The cause(s) of otosclerosis are not clear, although observations that the disorder spans family generations make a genetic source likely.

The diminished hearing that occurs is not sudden. Rather, the change is gradual and is usually recognized when the person becomes aware that she or he can no longer hear a low-pitched sound such as a whisper. . . .

Tinnitus

Tinnitus is a ringing noise or other sound that occurs in the absence of an external source of sound. For some, tinnitus is an infrequent occurrence. Others are very inconvenienced by near-constant tinnitus. The noises experienced in tinnitus range in description and include electronic noise, hissing steam, chirping crickets, bells, breaking glass, buzzing, and even the noise of a chainsaw. The noises can be constant or may rise and fall in volume with head motion or with the planting of feet during running.

Tinnitus has various known triggers. Foods such as red wine, cheese, and chocolate have been implicated. Over-the-counter drugs such as ibuprofen and extra-strength aspirin, and prescribed drugs, including oral contraceptives and aminoglycoside antibiotics, can cause tinnitus. Drug-related tinnitus disappears when the dosage is reduced or the drug stopped. The growth of certain tumors can cause tinnitus.

The aging of the inner ear is also a factor in tinnitus. As nerve cells deteriorate and the many hairs in the cochlea that transmit sound waves to the nerves become damaged and broken with time, the signaling of sound impulses to the brain becomes faulty. Nerves may fire when there has been no stimulus. The brain interprets the signal as actual noise.

Sudden hearing loss

This rapid decrease or complete loss of hearing can occur within minutes or over the course of several days. The hearing loss typically affects one ear and often resolves with time. Sudden deafness is much more serious and should be treated as a medical emergency requiring immediate medical attention. Causes are unclear and may revolve an infection, head injury, reaction to a drug, problems with circulation, and other disorders such as multiple sclerosis.

Deafness

The complete loss of hearing can be due to genetically determined developmental difficulties, a trauma such as a loud noise, physical damage to structures in the ear, nerves, or relevant areas of the brain, and infection during pregnancy (such as rubella). In a great many cases, deafness is permanent. Childhood deafness typically becomes apparent when a child appears inattentive and fails to meet language milestones.

> **FAST FACT**
>
> According to the National Institute on Deafness and Other Communication Disorders, the rate of hearing loss rises with age: 18 percent of American adults 45–64 years old, 30 percent of adults 65–74 years old, and 47 percent of adults 75 years old or older have a hearing impairment.

Diagnosis

Presbycusis is usually first detected by a family physician. Diagnosis is subsequently made by a hearing specialist or an audiologist, and involves a hearing test in which sounds of differing frequencies and gradually decreasing volume are sent to one ear at a time.

Tinnitus is self-evident, as the ringing or other sensation is impossible to ignore. In contrast, otitis media can be difficult to diagnose, as it is often not accompanied by

The Higher the Decibels, the Quicker the Hearing Loss Occurs

Sound Level	Exposure Limit
85 dB (A)	8 hours
88 dB (A)	4 hours
91 dB (A)	2 hours
94 dB (A)	1 hour
97 dB (A)	30 minutes
100 dB (A)	15 minutes
103 dB (A)	7.5 minutes
106 dB (A)	3.75 minutes

Taken from: US Army Center for Health Promotion and Preventative Medicine, "Hearing and Hearing Loss Prevention." http://chppm-www.apgea.army.mil/hcp/hhlp.aspx.

pain or a fever. Fluid in the ear can be a sign of otitis media. Also, changes in children's behavior such as playing the television louder, misunderstanding directions, and pulling at the ears can all be indicators of otitis media. . . .

Treatment

Treatment for presbycusis can be as simple as keeping the ear canals free from sound-muffling wax buildup. Another fairly common treatment for older people is the use of a hearing aid, which amplifies sound and directs the sound into the ear canal. About 20% of those with age-related hearing loss can benefit from an aid. More severe presbycusis can be treated using a cochlear implant. The device actually compensates for the nonworking parts of the inner ear. Conductive hearing loss can usually be fully corrected by medication or surgery. Similarly, when tinnitus is caused by overmedication, the condition is alleviated by modifying or eliminating the dosage of the drug. . . .

Otosclerosis that is more pronounced can be treated by a surgical procedure called a stapedectomy, in which the damaged portion of the middle ear, the stapes, one of the three bones of the middle ear, is bypassed by an implanted device that routes sound to the inner ear. Milder otosclerosis may be lessened by the use of a hearing aid.

Some conditions that can be addressed by surgery or the use of a hearing aid or an implant have varying levels of recovery. Other conditions involving permanent deafness cannot be cured.

As of April 2004, at least eight [hearing-related] clinical trials were active in the United States. Most focus on deafness, in particular the determination of the genetic factors that contribute to or cause deafness. . . .

Outlook for Recovery

Age-related hearing loss can be partially or almost completely compensated for by a change in lifestyle and the development of coping skills (listening to the radio at higher volume, different conversational behavior in crowds, use of hearing aids or implants). Otitis media can cause delayed speech development, if undiagnosed, because of the child's impaired ability to hear. Sudden hearing loss usually resolves on its own within a few days to several weeks. However, in about 15% of cases, the condition worsens with time.

The various surgeries that can be performed all carry some risk, and the quality of sound that is provided by cochlear implants varies greatly among recipients.

Hearing Loss Can Upset Balance as Well as Communication

Susan Schwerin

Infections and other assaults on the ear lead to more than just difficulties in hearing. In the following viewpoint neuroscientist Susan Schwerin describes how ear infections can wreak havoc in multiple ways. The buildup of pressure from pus and other fluids can cause the eardrum to burst. Apart from the excruciating pain of such infections, the aftermath can be worse. Infection can spread into brain tissue, Schwerin writes. It can also attack the vestibular organs of the inner ear, which govern the sense of orientation and equilibrium. That can leave a person feeling constantly dizzy and unable to balance upright. Schwerin is a doctoral candidate in neuroscience at Northwestern University.

Although its most obvious role is in hearing, the auditory system contains organs that mediate both hearing and balance. Problems in the auditory system can range from a simple ear ache to complete deafness and may also involve difficulties with equilib-

SOURCE: Susan Schwerin, "Hearing Disorders," *Posit Science,* March 29, 2009. Reproduced by permission.

rium. Each type of pathology is the result of damage in a specific part of the auditory system. Common pathologies of the auditory system are ear aches, hearing loss, ringing of the ears, and vestibular [balance] disturbances.

Many of us have experienced an auditory pathology called an ear ache, which is a dull pain in the ears. Ear aches are caused by problems in either the outer ear (the ear canal) or the middle ear (on the interior side of the ear drum). Both types of ear aches can usually be cured with antibiotics. Inflammation of the outer ear is called otitis externa and is caused by infection or physical injury of the ear canal. Some of the more common sources of otitis externa are bacteria or fungi entering the ear through shower water or swimming pool water. Otitis externa may also result from bacteria infecting sites of physical injury, such as injuries caused by scraping the ear canal with a fingernail or a cotton swab. These infections can be quite painful, but again treatment with antibiotics is effective.

Pressure Builds During Infection

Infection is also the culprit in middle ear pain (otitis media). The infection is often a complication accompanying upper respiratory disorder. In otitis media, bacteria or viruses infect the middle ear, causing a swelling which blocks a eustachian tube. The eustachian tubes are a pair of thin passageways that connect each middle ear to the back of the throat. They are closed most of the time, but open briefly over a thousand times a day during swallowing to drain the middle ears and to equalize the air pressure on both sides of the ear drum. When the eustachian tube is blocked by swelling during an infection, pus and other fluids cannot drain from the middle ear, and so these fluids accumulate and put painful pressure on the ear drum. A blocked eustachian tube can also cause pain during changes in external air pressure, such as changes that occur when riding in elevators or planes. Otitis media can be diagnosed with a tympanogram, a record of

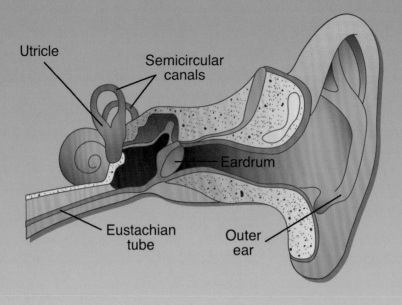

Inner Ear and Balance

Utricle

Semicircular canals

Eardrum

Eustachian tube

Outer ear

Taken from: www.mayoclinic.com.

the movements of the ear drum. Normally, the ear drum sways in and out in response to an air puff or sound wave, but if fluid has accumulated on the internal side of the ear drum, these oscillations are dampened. Because the ear drum cannot vibrate normally, sounds seem muffled or faint. With proper treatment and antibiotics, hearing can be restored.

While most cases of middle ear infection are straightforward, there can be complications. In some cases the pressure within the ear is high enough to cause the thin membrane of the ear drum to rupture. The trapped fluids then drain out of the ear and the pain diminishes. The body can usually repair a hole or tear in the ear drum naturally, but sometimes a skin graft (tympanoplasty) is required to close the perforation. Occasionally the body's natural repair mechanisms can go awry, and as tears in the ear drum heal, the membrane continues to grow into

PERSPECTIVES ON DISEASES AND DISORDERS

the middle ear, developing into a benign tumor called a cholesteatoma. This cholesteatoma can erode the bones of the middle ear, potentially causing infections of brain tissue. Such complications underscore the importance of early and effective treatment for cholesteatoma. Physicians typically treat the infection first, and then surgically remove the middle ear tumor.

Children Succumb Easily

Ear infections are particularly prevalent amongst young children; in fact, ear infections are second only to the common cold in bringing children to the doctor's office. Children with recurring, or chronic infections may be treated by the insertion of drainage tubes into the ear. For this procedure, a hole is cut in the ear drum and a tiny tube is threaded in. The tube allows drainage of the middle ear and also allows the air pressure to equalize. The tubes stay in the ear for 6 months to 3 years and fall out by themselves. Early treatment of hearing loss in children is very important to ensure proper speech and language development.

In addition to infection, hearing loss might result from head injuries, loud noise, wax buildup, or aging. Physicians group all of these forms of hearing loss into three main categories based on the site of damage; thus, hearing loss can be sensorineural, conductive or cortical. . . .

Some types of damage to the auditory system cause problems beyond hearing loss. Ringing in the ears is an auditory system pathology called tinnitus that often accompanies hearing loss. Researchers believe that tinnitus is caused by damage to the auditory nerve endings in the cochlea. The most common cause of this type of damage is exposure to loud noise, although normal aging and some infections can also trigger tinnitus. While there is no cure for tinnitus, high volume white noise, like static, can be used to mask the disturbing ringing.

FAST FACT

Although infection is the most common cause of loss of balance and dizziness, they can also be symptoms of multiple sclerosis, a far more significant and incurable disease.

Loss of Balance

Finally, damage to the auditory system can affect one's sense of balance and position. The anatomy of the inner ear is involved in maintaining equilibrium as well as in hearing. The vestibular organs in the inner ear include two swellings called the utricle and saccule, and the three semicircular canals. Sensory cells within this group of organs respond to the direction and speed of head motion and to head position. Problems with these organs can result in vestibular symptoms including dizziness, nausea and imbalance. Benign Paroxysmal Positional Vertigo (BPPV) is a type of vestibular condition that arises from the free movement of small crystals in the inner ear that are ordinarily attached to the nerve endings. Normal degeneration or exposure to loud sounds can detach the

Ear infections are most prevalent among young children, second only to the common cold. **(Mark Clarke/Photo Researchers, Inc.)**

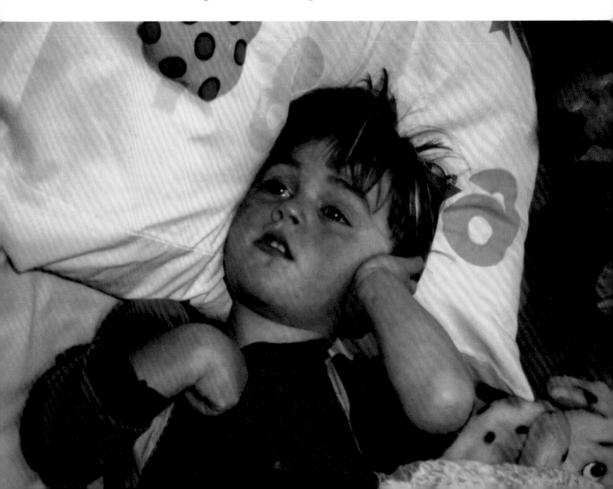

crystals from the nerve endings. These crystals, sometimes called "ear rocks," can block the semicircular canals when the head is moved, resulting in vestibular symptoms. Treatment is aimed at transferring the crystals to a less sensitive location by moving the head through a specific sequence of positions. Often, infections or abnormalities in the inner ear affect both hearing and equilibrium, and difficulties with both are observed.

In conclusion, abnormalities in auditory system function can cause difficulties in hearing as well as balance. Preventative measures, such as avoiding loud noises, refraining from putting anything in the ear, and promptly treating infections will help to protect auditory function for years to come.

Loud Music Induces Hearing Loss

Bernard Perusse

The rise of rock and roll brought with it a new health hazard: music-induced hearing loss. In this article Canadian journalist Bernard Perusse puts the issue in perspective through interviews with a number of people in the rock music industry who have suffered hearing loss. The victims range from performers who lost some hearing and have invested in high-tech protective ear-wear to a man who had to give up his job as president of a prestigious record company as a result of his increasing deafness. Perusse also profiles a company that is marketing products to prevent noise-induced damage to the ears. Perusse reports for the *Montreal Gazette*. He also reviews rock-related media on Amazon.com.

The wake-up call for Jonas came three years ago [in 2004]. The Montreal rocker, who now cranks out the kind of volume required of a Bell Centre headliner was decompressing after a show with his guitarist and right-hand man, Corey Diabo. "We were in a hotel room, talking, and we could barely hear each other," said Jonas, 28. "We just heard the hissing and buzzing in our ears. We were noticing that it would last until the next day in soundcheck—sometimes two days later. We were tired of it."

The two performers began looking for ways to protect their hearing and finally settled on in-ear monitors, which allow musicians to bypass the punishing loudness of large stage monitors or onstage speakers and hear what they're playing directly through an earphone. With "in-ears," each musician receives his own personal mix—more bass, more crowd, more guitar, as needed—from a sound engineer, who transmits it to the performer's wireless belt pack, connected to the earphone. The net result is that each band member can now hear his or her performance at a reasonable volume.

Jonas recently had his hearing tested. "The results were really quite positive," he said. "It's not 100 percent, that's for sure. There's been some damage, but (the audiologist) said to keep going the way I'm going and take the precautions."

Young People Are Losing Hearing

Long dismissed by the youth demographic as an old person's problem, hearing loss now affects people earlier. According to the Canadian Hearing Society, nearly one in four Canadians report having a hearing loss. Of those, nearly one in four are under 40. A poll commissioned [in 2006] by the American Speech-Language-Hearing Association concluded that more than half of American high-school students surveyed reported some signs of hearing loss.

Until recently, though, hearing loss was rock 'n' roll's dirty little secret. In the 1970s, Who leader Pete Townshend went public about his struggles with tinnitus, a persistent noise-induced ringing in the ears, but, mostly, the rock community's silence on the subject was itself deafening.

In 1988, Townshend donated $10,000 to musician Kathy Peck's H.E.A.R. (Hearing Education and Awareness for Rockers), a San Francisco–based grassroots organization and advocacy group that seeks to inform not only musicians, but also the public at large, about ways to prevent the permanent hearing loss facing post-rock generations. Among other things, H.E.A.R. refers inquirers to audiologists, provides ear protection and has helped pass a San Francisco ordinance requiring concert venues to distribute free earplugs. The organization has steadily gained a higher profile, becoming a chief representative of rock's out-of-the-closet concerns about going deaf.

Peck was playing bass in the Contractions, a Frisco all-female punk band, when her music career was cut short. She can pretty much put a date on it. "We opened for Duran Duran at the Oakland Coliseum in '84," she said in a telephone interview. "It was so loud from the screaming little girls that I experienced ringing in my ears for about three or four days. It was constant and really severe. After that show, my hearing dropped significantly, to the point where I couldn't hear people speak."

Rockers Are at Risk

Marshall Chasin, director of auditory research at the Musicians Clinics of Canada in Toronto, said nine out of 10 musicians he sees—who have been referred after experiencing other problems, like back injuries—have the beginnings of a noise- or music-induced hearing loss. Many are classical musicians, he said, "but we see rockers anywhere between their teens and their 80s. And we see as many music listeners as music players."

Part of the challenge in bringing about an evolution in consciousness about rock-induced noise hazards, Peck said, is the marketplace emphasis on rehabilitation and the sale of expensive hearing aids. "After it's broken, we

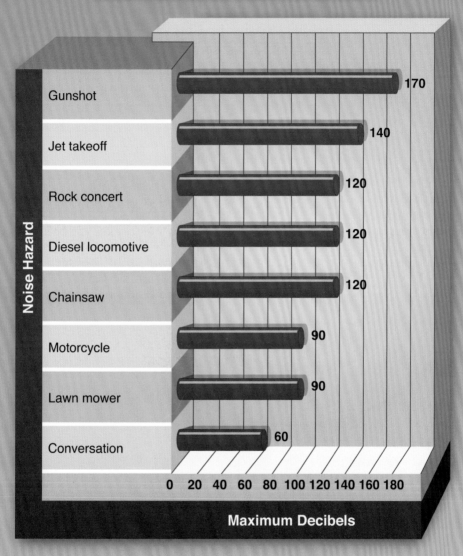

Rock Concerts Are Among the Highest Noise Hazards

Noise Hazard

Gunshot	170
Jet takeoff	140
Rock concert	120
Diesel locomotive	120
Chainsaw	120
Motorcycle	90
Lawn mower	90
Conversation	60

0 20 40 60 80 100 120 140 160 180

Maximum Decibels

Taken from: Peter M. Rabinowitz, "Noise-Induced Hearing Loss," *American Family Physician*, May 1, 2000.

fix it," she said. "That's what makes money for the companies. They're providing a product, but we're preventing something. That's not going to give anybody business."

[Entrepreneur] Nick Laperle is looking to change that, for both musicians and simple music lovers. He made his decision in 1994, when he decided not to take over the successful hearing-aid practice started by his mother, Mary Jane Gaudet. "Hearing aids are an after-fix. Can't we do something better than that? Can't we prevent hearing loss? It's the No. 1 occupational illness. How come no one's paying attention?" he remembers saying to her. Laperle's own answer to those questions was to launch Sonomax, which offers customized ear protection.

Customized Ear Protection

Musicians are a significant part of Sonomax's clientele, but any customer can have protection earpieces molded specifically to his or her ears. The earpieces, which are immediately tested for their ability to keep sound out,

Rocker Pete Townshend, right, of the rock group The Who, went public about his hearing loss and increased awareness of hearing loss among rock musicians. (**AP Images**)

are ready in about 10 minutes. A filter is applied during the process, but its strength can be tailored to how much sound the customer needs to keep out.

With personal listening devices like iPods being a chief contributor to hearing loss among young people, Sonomax is launching a similar custom process for earphones that will be usable with iPods and other MP3 players and almost any audio device with an intra-ear application. The company promises not only better sound, but also an acoustic seal that blocks all competing noise, allowing the listener to keep the volume considerably lower.

Sonomax has recently signed a deal with Virgin Entertainment to sell the earphones in its megastores in New York City and Los Angeles, starting early [in 2008]. It also hopes to have kiosks in high-traffic malls soon. In the long term, Laperle said, the company would like to have a presence in a variety of audio retail outlets, where customers could be fitted on the spot.

This will be welcome news for iPod devotees like Jake Shenker, a 22-year-old musician who has been taking ear protection seriously since his father insisted he buy his first pair of drugstore earplugs when he joined his first rock band at the age of 12. Since he was 18, Shenker has used them regularly—even when attending loud shows.

Shenker acknowledged that his iPod habit is the biggest threat to his ears. "As soon as I get on the métro [subway], I can max the volume on my iPod and hear my music, but there's no way I can do it and not be in pain," he said. Laperle explained that the type of earbuds that come with devices like iPods are their weakest link. Their one-size generic model doesn't fit 80 per cent of users, and it lets in far too many other sounds, like traffic, the bus or the métro. The user's only option is to jack up the volume to a dangerous level to compete with the non-musical noise. "Your ear doesn't make the distinction that you're trying to increase your audio experience," Laperle said. "All it's measuring is the output." In other words, throw the métro noise on top of an iPod at max, and you're in trouble.

Hearing Loss Ends a Career

Dan Beck was among those who paid a high price for years of overexposure to rock 'n' roll: in 1999, he felt obliged to quit his job as president of North American operations for V2 Records, a label launched by industry mogul Richard Branson. "Here I was, working for the most enjoyable, wonderful billionaire in the world, with this wonderful staff and millions to spend in developing the label. You could not have asked for a greater situation in life to be in. It was everything I'd worked for," said Beck, 57. "But I felt I had hit the wall."

The record company executive discovered he had lost about 70 per cent of his mid-range hearing through a combination of exposure to loud music and genetic predisposition. His inability to hear other speakers at business meetings could no longer be blamed on allergy-caused congestion or transatlantic flights that had blocked his ears.

FAST FACT

iPods and other in-ear MP3 players are capable of producing ear-damaging volumes of over 100 decibels.

"I felt extremely vulnerable. I was working for this young, upstart company—and the president has hearing aids! And, frankly, that could be used against you in negotiations. Other record companies would say (to an artist), 'Oh, you're going to sign with that label with the guy with the hearing aids,'" he said, laughing. But getting the aids, Beck said, was the best thing he could have done. "People let it go, and they lose connection. And you lose connection, you're losing humanity. You're losing relationships," he said.

Laperle used similar logic when asked about a macho culture in the rock community, which manifests itself as a fear of seeming uncool by wearing protection. "It's not macho and it's not cool when you can't communicate with your girlfriend anymore," he said.

Beck, whose current company, Big Honcho Media, does promotional work for big-name clients like HBO, Fox and Universal Pictures, used his music-biz contacts to produce an educational video titled *Listen Smart* in 2002. The brief, high-energy film features rockers like Ozzy Osbourne, Moby, Debbie Harry, Metallica's Lars Ulrich and Brad Delson of Linkin Park telling their stories and urging teenage consumers to protect their hearing.

Newborns Should Be Screened for Potential Hearing Problems

Jace Wolfe and Walter Nance

Deafness in newborns is often hard to detect. In the following article two hearing specialists advocate widespread use of blood tests for newborns to detect molecular indications of hearing disorders. In cases where deafness is suspected, authors Jace Wolfe and Walter Nance strongly recommend testing to identify the cause. The simple and inexpensive blood tests can identify precisely what genetic mutation or viral infection is responsible, they say. This can have several benefits, according to Wolfe and Nance. Parents may find relief in knowing exactly what causes their child's deafness. Additionally, counseling may help them deal with the child's disability as well as avoid a recurrence with another child. Wolfe is director of audiology at the Hearts for Hearing Foundation in Oklahoma City. Nance is a research professor in the Department of Human Genetics at Virginia Commonwealth University School of Medicine.

SOURCE: Jace Wolfe and Walter Nance, "Molecular Screening for Children with Hearing Loss: Why Do It?" *ASHA Leader,* November 6, 2007, pp. 20–23. © American Speech-Language-Hearing Association, 2007. Reproduced by permission of the publisher and Jace Wolfe.

Recent estimates suggest that screening for a relatively small number of genetic and environmental causes for hearing loss in newborns will identify the etiology [cause] for as many as 70% of those who either have congenital [at birth] hearing loss or are at risk for late-onset pre-lingual [before speech] hearing loss. Screening tests for the relevant causes of deafness are already commercially available. All newborn infants would require screening to detect pre-symptomatic infants at risk for delayed-onset pre-linguistic hearing loss, but the tests can also be used in infants with identified hearing losses. As is true of most genetic tests, a positive test result would provide a reliable indication of the cause of hearing loss in an infant who is deaf, but a negative test result would not exclude other mutations or other genetic or environmental causes.

Molecular screening tests require a small sample of the child's blood, which is mailed to any one of several laboratories that offer tests for one or more of the following conditions: Connexin 26, Connexin 30, Pendred syndrome, the mitochondrial A1555T mutation, and cytomegalovirus (CMV). Screening results typically are reported within 48 hours of specimen receipt. To exclude congenital CMV infection as the cause for hearing loss, however, the blood sample must be obtained within the first few weeks of life.

Screening for these specific causes of deafness provide an affordable method to detect the most common causes of congenital and delayed-onset pre-lingual deafness. Families in which the probable cause for the hearing loss is identified should seek professional advice from primary care physicians, geneticists, otolaryngologists [ear, nose, and throat specialists], or experts in infectious disease, if appropriate, for a full evaluation and counseling about the significance of test results. In cases of negative test results, parents interested in a more thorough assessment of possible genetic mutations associated with congenital hearing loss should see a geneticist for a diagnostic assessment.

One may ask why it is important for a clinician to know the etiology of a pediatric patient's hearing loss. The answer is clear—knowing the cause of a child's hearing loss may improve clinicians' abilities to provide gold-standard service.

Parents' Concerns

A [2002] survey by [medical researchers Melody] Roush and [Jackson] Harrison asked parents what information they would like to receive pertaining to their child's hearing loss. Parents reported their most pressing concern at the time of initial diagnosis was the cause of their child's hearing loss. Based upon personal experience, some parents noted that uncertainty regarding the cause of hearing loss at the time of diagnosis made it more difficult to address intervention issues. Other families noted that they worried about the cause of hearing loss for years after the initial diagnosis and often erroneously associated the hearing loss with something innocuous during pregnancy, such as drinking too many caffeinated beverages. One mother expressed relief when genetic screening revealed her 3-year-old son's hearing loss was attributed to a Connexin 26 mutation. She had never before revealed her fear that the loss was due to an over-the-counter decongestant taken during pregnancy.

Parents often feel guilty about their child's hearing loss when they learn of the cause. As part of genetic counseling, a geneticist can explain that everyone carries abnormal genes. In the case of recessive traits, which include most—but not all—causes of deafness, it is only when both parents carry the same "weak" gene that a child risks inheriting a "double dose" of the gene and becoming deaf. A genetic diagnosis includes important implications concerning the hearing status of future children. In whatever way the parents decide to use this in-

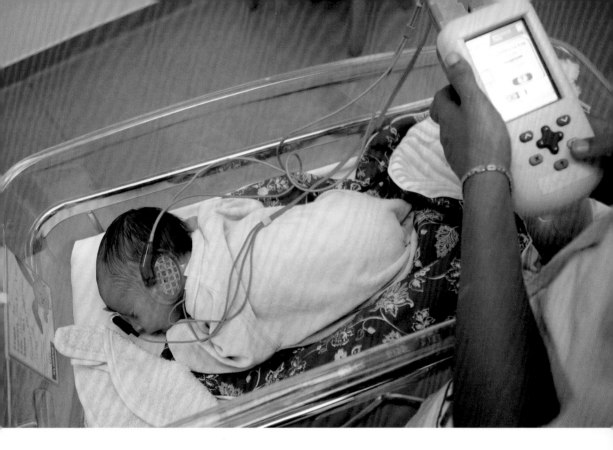

formation, they will not again face the totally unexpected birth of a child who is deaf, and most families are relieved to know the cause and its implications.

In any pediatric patient with pre-lingual hearing loss of unknown cause, audiologists should routinely document that they have urged the parents to seek genetic counseling. For other genetic diseases, physicians have sometimes been held liable for assuring their patients that "lightning never strikes twice."

Because deafness in infants is hard to detect, hearing tests for newborns may not be enough. (Olivier Voisin/Photo Researchers, Inc.)

Indicators for Cochlear Implants

Although some studies have indicated that the etiology of hearing loss does not necessarily limit receiving a benefit from such hearing technology as a cochlear implant, some particular diagnoses—such as Connexin 26 mutations and Pendred syndrome—typically are associated with good outcomes for cochlear implantation. Thus, a family may feel more comfortable about moving forward

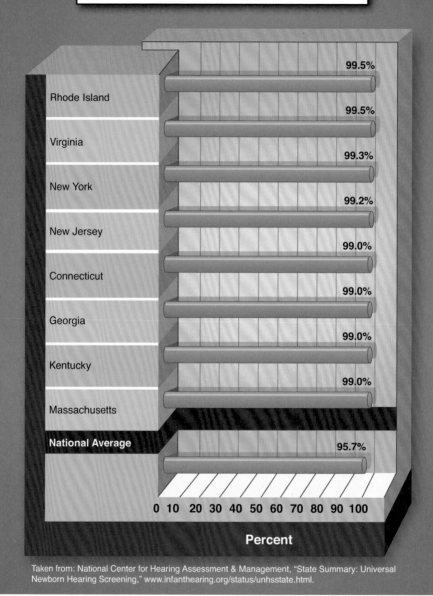

Leading States in Newborn Hearing Screening, 2006

State	Percent
Rhode Island	99.5%
Virginia	99.5%
New York	99.3%
New Jersey	99.2%
Connecticut	99.0%
Georgia	99.0%
Kentucky	99.0%
Massachusetts	99.0%
National Average	95.7%

Percent: 0 10 20 30 40 50 60 70 80 90 100

Taken from: National Center for Hearing Assessment & Management, "State Summary: Universal Newborn Hearing Screening," www.infanthearing.org/status/unhsstate.html.

with cochlear implantation knowing that it has provided favorable outcomes for others with the same type of hearing loss as their child.

Additionally, cochlear implants are now advocated for children as young as 6 months of age. Assessment of

PERSPECTIVES ON DISEASES AND DISORDERS

minimal response levels to acoustic stimuli is challenging when working with children with hearing loss during their first few months of life. The recommendation of a cochlear implant for children less than 1 year old may be based at least partially upon electrophysiological assessment. Inclusion of genetic screening into the assessment battery may provide knowledge of the etiology of the hearing loss, which—along with electrophysiological assessment and the subjective report of the child's family and speech-language pathologist—allows cochlear implant teams to make better-informed recommendations of cochlear implantation for children under 1 year old.

For example, electrophysiological results consistent with profound hearing loss, along with a finding of a Connexin 26 mutation, would support the recommendation of cochlear implantation at an early age. Moreover, anecdotal experience has suggested that some pediatricians are not convinced by results of electrophysiologic assessments that indicate permanent congenital hearing loss. The diagnosis of such a hearing loss is met with much less skepticism when it is accompanied by unequivocal genetic evidence.

Screening Guides Treatment Plan

Knowledge of certain etiologies also may change the management of services provided for a child with hearing loss. For example, Pendred syndrome is typically associated with an enlarged vestibular aqueduct, an anatomical abnormality that often results in fluctuating or progressive hearing loss. Consequently, frequent audiologic assessments should be conducted to characterize the degree and configuration of the child's hearing loss and to ensure hearing aids are fitted appropriately.

The increased likelihood of a fluctuating/progressive hearing loss may influence the choice of amplification provided for a child given the need for flexible electroacoustic characteristics to account for possible changes in hearing sensitivity. In addition, downward progression of hearing sensitivity associated with enlarged vestibular aqueduct is frequently coincident with physical trauma and/or barotrauma [pressure-induced trauma], so families can be counseled to avoid activities that may place the child at risk (i.e. contact sports or scuba diving).

CMV is one of the leading causes of acquired congenital hearing loss in the United States. Most people are infected with CMV after the neonatal period and have no signs or symptoms. However, when CMV is contracted in utero, serious neurological and sensory deficits, including hearing loss, may occur. The only way to determine if a child's hearing loss is attributable to CMV is to screen for the virus in the neonatal period, specifically within the first two to three weeks of life.

The neurological deficits associated with congenital CMV often result in serious cognitive, speech, and language delays. When congenital CMV is confirmed as the probable etiology for congenital hearing loss, hearing health care professionals are better-equipped to discuss a prognosis for development of speech, language, and auditory skills. In this country [USA], unilateral deafness—which is most commonly caused by CMV—is considered to be a clinically significant abnormality because of substantial evidence that as a group, children with unilateral deafness exhibit poor school performance. Additional intervention may be proactively identified and provided to address possible cognitive delay. . . .

Screening for CMV—which is responsible for up to 25% of congenital hearing loss—must take place within the first few weeks of life to determine whether the infection is congenital or acquired. Infections acquired postnatally are typically asymptomatic, while congenital CMV may cause serious disabilities, such as hearing loss, visual impairment, and neurologic abnormalities, but in

FAST FACT

Hearing loss is one of the most common congenital anomalies, occurring in approximately 2 to 4 infants per 1,000.

other affected infants, hearing loss is the only recognized abnormality. When a physician knows an infant has congenital CMV, various assessments may be ordered in a timely fashion and early intervention may be provided.

Hearing health care providers should [be] expanding the traditional battery of assessments to include the provision of molecular screening for children with hearing loss. Knowledge of the etiology of the hearing loss is appreciated by families and improves intervention services.

Hearing Aids Help Those with Hearing Loss

Carol A. Turkington

Just as people with vision impairment wear glasses, many people with hearing impairment wear hearing aids. In the following article writer Carol A. Turkington explains how the devices work and what the advantages and disadvantages of various types of hearing aids may be. All hearing aids have certain features in common, such as a microphone, amplifier, and power source, she explains. However, they vary widely in size, power, and arrangement in the ear. Turkington is a medical writer. She has published articles in numerous national magazines and has authored or edited more than twenty books on medical and health issues.

A hearing aid is a device that can amplify sound waves in order to help a deaf or hard-of-hearing person hear sounds more clearly. Recent technology can help most people with hearing loss understand speech better and achieve better communication.

SOURCE: Carol A. Turkington, *Gale Encyclopedia of Medicine*, Detroit, MI: Gale, 2006. Copyright © 2006 Gale, a part of Cengage Learning Inc. All rights reserved. Reproduced by permission of Gale, a part of Cengage Learning.

It's important that a person being fitted for a hearing aid understand what an aid can and can't do. An aid can help a person hear better, but it won't return hearing to normal levels. Hearing aids boost all sounds, not just those the person wishes to hear. Especially when the source of sound is far away (such as up on a stage), environmental noise can interfere with good speech perception. And while the aid amplifies sound, it doesn't necessarily improve the clarity of the sound. A hearing aid is a machine, and can never duplicate the true sound that people with normal hearing experience, but it will help the person take advantage of the hearing that remains.

More than 1,000 different models are available in the United States. All of them include a microphone (to pick up sound), amplifier (to boost sound strength), a receiver or speaker (to deliver sound to the ear), and are powered by a battery. Depending on the style, it's possible to add features to filter or block out background noise, minimize feedback, lower sound in noisy settings, or boost power when needed.

Types of Hearing Aids

Hearing aids are either "monaural" (a hearing aid for one ear), or "binaural" (for two ears); more than 65% of all users have binaural aids. Hearing aids are divided into several different types:

- digital
- in-the-ear
- in-the-canal
- behind-the-ear
- on-the-body

Digital Aids

Digital aids are sophisticated, very expensive aids that borrow computer technology to allow a person to tailor an aid to a specific hearing loss pattern. Using miniature computer chips, the aids can selectively boost certain frequencies while leaving others alone. This means a person could wear such an aid to a loud party, and screen out unwanted background noise, while tuning in on one-on-one conversations. The aid is programmed by the dealer to conform to the patient's specific hearing loss. Some models can be programmed to allow the wearer to choose different settings depending on the noise of the environment.

In-the-Ear Aids

In-the-ear aids are lightweight devices whose custom-made housings contain all the components; this device fits into the ear canal with no visible wires or tubes. It's possible to control tone but not volume with these aids, so they are helpful only for people with mild hearing loss. Some people find these aids are easier to put on and take off than behind-the-ear aids. However, because they are custom-fit to a person's ear, it is not possible to try on before ordering. Some people find them uncomfortable in hot weather.

In-the-Canal Aids

In-the-canal aids fit far into the ear canal, with only a small bit extending into the external ear. The smallest is the MicroCanal, which fits out of sight down next to the eardrum and is removed with a small transparent wire. These are extremely expensive, but they are not visible, offer better acoustics, and are easier to maintain. They can more closely mimic natural sound because of the position of the microphone; this position also cuts down on wind noise. But their small size makes them harder to handle, and their battery is especially small and difficult to insert. Adjusting the volume may be hard, since a person must stick a finger down into the ear to adjust volume, and this very tiny aid doesn't have the power of other, larger, aids.

Behind-the-Ear Aids

Behind-the-ear aids include a microphone, amplifier and receiver inside a small curved case worn behind the ear; the case is connected to the earmold by a short plastic tube.

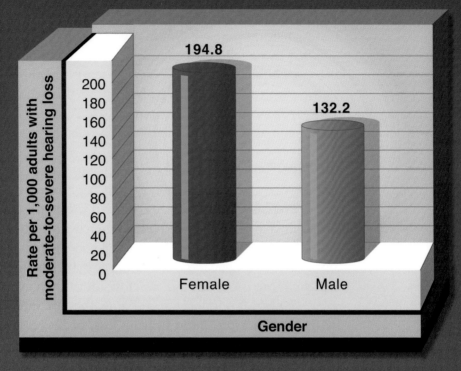

More Women than Men Make Use of Hearing Aids

194.8

132.2

Rate per 1,000 adults with moderate-to-severe hearing loss

200
180
160
140
120
100
80
60
40
20
0

Female

Male

Gender

Taken from: NIDCD, "Use of Hearing Aids in 2001," June 11, 2008. www.nidcd.nih.gov/health/statistics/hearingaids.

The earmold extends into the ear canal. Some models have both tone and volume control, plus a telephone pickup device. However, many users think them unattractive and out of date; and people who wear glasses find that the glasses interfere with the aid's fit. Others don't have space behind the ear for the mold to fit comfortably. However, they do offer a few advantages. Behind-the-ear aids:

- don't require as much maintenance
- are easily interchangeable if they need to be serviced
- are more powerful
- are easier to handle than smaller aids
- can provide better sound quality
- tend to be more reliable

Eyeglass Models

Eyeglass models are the same as behind-the-ear devices, except that the case fits into an eyeglass frame instead of resting behind the ears. Not many people buy this type of aid, but those who do believe it's less obvious, although there is a tube that travels from the temple of the glasses to the earmold. But it can be hard to fit this type of aid, and repairs can be problematic. Also, if the aid breaks, the person also loses the benefit of the glasses. . . .

On-the-Body Aids

On-the-body aids feature a larger microphone, amplifier, and power supply inside a case carried inside the pocket, or attached to clothing. The receiver attaches directly to the earmold; its power comes through a flexible wire from the amplifier. Although larger than other aids, the on-the-body aids are more powerful and easier to adjust than other devices. While not popular for everyone, they are often used by those with a profound hearing loss, or by very young children. Some people who are almost totally deaf find they need the extra power boost available only from a body aid.

Next-Generation Aids

The latest aids on the market may eliminate the amplifier and speaker in favor of a tiny magnet mounted on a silicone disk, similar to a contact lens, which rests right on the eardrum. Called the Earlens, it is designed to be held in place by a thin film of oil. Users wear a wireless microphone, either in the ear or on a necklace, that picks up sounds and converts them into magnetic signals, making the magnet vibrate. As the Earlens vibrates, so does the eardrum, transmitting normal-sounding tones to the middle and inner ears.

Other researchers are bypassing the middle ear completely; they surgically implant a tiny magnet in the inner ear. By attaching a magnet to the round window, they open a second pathway to the inner ear. An electromag-

Hearing aids are usually used (clockwise, bottom left to right) in the ear, behind the ear, or in the ear canal. (**BSIP/ Photo Researchers, Inc.**)

netic coil implanted in bone behind the ear vibrates the implanted magnet. Unlike the Earlens, this magnetic implant would not block the normal hearing pathway.

Exam and Evaluation

The first step in getting a hearing aid is to have a medical exam and a hearing evaluation. (Most states prohibit anyone selling a hearing aid until the patient has been examined by a physician to rule out medical problems.) After performing a hearing evaluation, an audiologist should be able to determine whether a hearing aid will help, and which one will do the most good. This is especially important because aids can be very expensive (between $500 and $4,000), and are often not covered by health insurance. Hearing aids come in a wide range of styles and types, requiring careful testing to make sure the aid is the best choice for a particular hearing loss.

Some audiologists sell aids; others can make a recommendation, or give one a list of competent dealers in one's area. Patients should shop around and compare prices. In all but three states, hearing aids must be fitted and sold only by licensed specialists called dealers, specialists, dispensers, or dispensing audiologists.

The hearing aid dealer will make an impression of the consumer's ears using a putty-like material, from which a personalized earmold will be created. It's the dealer's job to make sure the aid fits properly. The person may need several visits to find the right hearing aid and learn how to use it. The dealer will help the consumer learn how to put the aid on, adjust the controls, and maintain the device. The dealer should be willing to service the aid and provide information about what to do if sensitivity to the earmold develops. (Some people are allergic to the materials in the mold.)

FAST FACT

According to the National Institute on Deafness and Other Communication Disorders, only one out of five people who could benefit from a hearing aid actually wears one.

Follow-Up

Within several weeks, the wearer should return to the dealer to have the aid checked, and to discuss the progress in wearing the aid. About 40% of all aids need some modification or adjustment in the beginning.

Within the first month of getting an aid, the patient should make an appointment for a full hearing examination to determine if the aid is functioning properly.

While there are no medical risks to hearing aids, there is a risk associated with hearing aids: many people end up not wearing their aids because they say everything seems loud when wearing them. This is because they have lived for so long with a hearing problem that they have forgotten how loud "normal" sound can be. Other potential problems with hearing aids include earmold discomfort, and a build up of excess ear wax after getting a hearing aid.

A hearing aid will boost the loudness of sound, which can improve a person's ability to understand speech.

Cochlear Implants Can Restore Hearing

Regina Nuzzo

Some kinds of hearing loss cannot be overcome by hearing aids. Just as those who are deaf cannot benefit from them, people who lose hearing in the upper ranges may find it impossible to follow human speech, because certain sounds just cannot be heard. Amplification via hearing aids does not remedy this situation. In the following viewpoint science journalist Regina Nuzzo describes how a new type of cochlear implant, known as a hybrid, can help. Traditional cochlear implants, she explains, destroy whatever is left of the natural hearing system and replace it with an electronic one. For deaf people, there is nothing to lose and much to be gained. However, for those who have partial hearing loss, the traditional device may be inappropriate. The hybrid cochlear implant, however, replaces only the high-pitched end of hearing. Together with a hearing aid, it can restore the ability to understand what people are saying—the most important hearing skill for most people.

Nuzzo is a science and health writer. She holds a bachelor's degree in engineering from the University of South Florida, earned a doctorate in statistics from Stanford University, and is a graduate of the University of California at Santa Cruz science writing program.

SOURCE: Regina Nuzzo, "A More Sound Solution," *Los Angeles Times*, December 11, 2006. Copyright © 2006 Los Angeles Times. Reproduced by permission.

Jeanne Yeoman had been dealing with her hearing loss for a couple of decades, but listening still exhausted her. And technology wasn't really helping her patience. She remembers driving down the road one day and coming close to just hurling her hearing aids out the window. "Hearing aids made everything louder, not clearer," she says. "I didn't need amplification. I needed clarification."

Yeoman wasn't deaf. So she was surprised to learn she was an ideal candidate for an experimental type of cochlear implant. Unlike hearing aids, cochlear implants communicate directly with the brain by converting sounds into electrical impulses and shooting them along the auditory nerve. Until now these devices have been used only for profoundly deaf people. But this new "hybrid" cochlear implant was designed specifically for partial hearing loss—so that users could enjoy both their own natural hearing plus bionic hearing for sounds where they need an extra boost.

Five years after surgery that implanted the device in her inner ear, 34-year-old Yeoman of Humboldt, Iowa, sometimes even forgets it's turned on. "Everything sounds so crystal-clear," she says.

FAST FACT

Cochlear implants do not come cheap. According to the National Association of the Deaf, the cost of the device and implantation surgery runs between $40,000 and $60,000.

When Hearing Aids Cannot Help Enough

Good solutions are scarce for many people with hearing loss, including growing numbers of aging baby boomers. A large number of the 28 million hard-of-hearing Americans have what is known as a "ski-slope" loss, in which their ability to hear high-pitched sounds plummets dramatically. They can hear sounds such as "aah" and "ooh" quite plainly, but not "ssss" or "shhh." Unfortunately, the latter types of sounds give speech the lion's share of its legibility. Speech doesn't necessarily sound quiet; it sounds muddy.

Even at full blast, hearing aids often can't help enough, says Dr. James Battey, director of the National Institute on Deafness and Other Communication Disorders at the National Institutes of Health. "This type of hearing loss can become extremely socially isolating," he says.

Traditional cochlear implants aren't a good answer. By bypassing damaged inner ears to stimulate auditory nerve fibers directly, these devices can be a boon for some deaf people. But the procedure—which involves threading a tiny bundle of electronics into the inner ear through a hole in the skull—aims to replace a patient's entire range of hearing. Any natural abilities usually get wiped out by the surgery.

Hybrid Implants Hold Promise

With the new hybrid implant, however, surgeons hope simply to supplement natural hearing without destroying

A surgeon at a microscope with a television monitor inserts a cochlear implant into a deaf patient's ear. (James King-Holmes/Photo Researchers, Inc.)

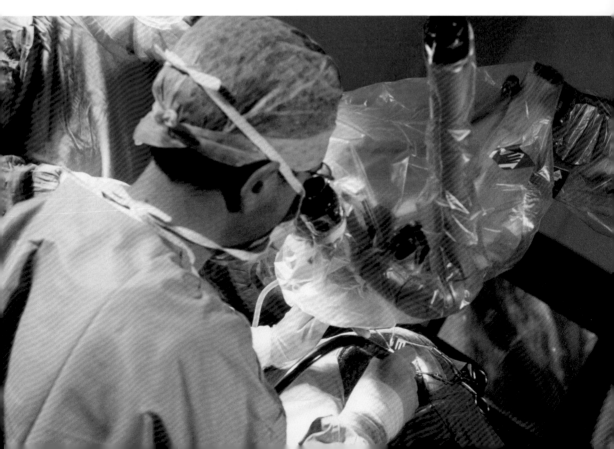

it, says Dr. Bruce Gantz, professor of otolaryngology at the University of Iowa and developer of the device.

The secret lies in the inner ear's design. Normal hearing is sort of a Rube Goldberg process. First, sound waves enter the ear as rhythmic pulses, which set the eardrum vibrating in sync. This triggers quivering in three tiny bones, with the last bone hammering against the entrance to the inner ear. In response, fluid sloshes in rhythmic waves throughout the corridors of the snail-shaped cochlea, which alerts sensory cells to electrically stimulate auditory nerve fibers.

Strangely enough, the cochlea itself is laid out like a coiled piano keyboard: Cells along the corridors are tuned to particular frequencies entering the ear. In the case of a low-pitched sound, cells tucked away deep inside the cochlea alert the auditory nerve; cells that respond to high notes sit close to the cochlea's entrance. That's fortunate—because cochlear regions where "ski-slope" patients need a boost are those most accessible to surgeons.

Compared with traditional implants, hybrid systems use a thinner, shorter bundle of electronics (10 millimeters in length compared with up to 28 millimeters for traditional implants). This short electrode is positioned just at the opening end of the cochlea, stimulating the auditory nerve only when high-frequency sound waves enter the ear. Since surgeons don't need to probe as deeply into the delicate cochlea, tissue trauma is reduced. Preserved natural hearing, amplified with a hearing aid if necessary, gives patients an easier time in tough situations, such as crowded restaurants or concert halls. The added high-frequency electronic hearing clears up muddy speech.

Clinical Trials

Since 1999, about 80 patients have received the hybrid device, Gantz says, and clinical trials are underway at

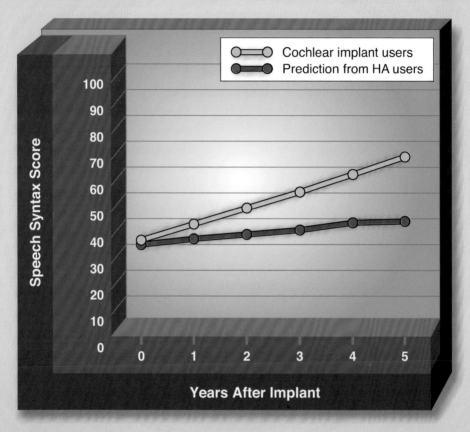

Speech Syntax Scores of Cochlear Implant Users Versus Hearing Aid Users

Cochlear implant users
Prediction from HA users

Speech Syntax Score

Years After Implant

Compiled by editor.

15 U.S. sites. Preliminary results, released in November [2006], reported that surgeons in the trial have been able to retain hearing in about 96% of the patients. Before surgery, patients were able to understand about one-third of words on standard hearing tests. After one year or more with the implant, scores increased to an average of 75%.

Hybrid implant users also function better than traditional implant users in noisy situations, says Christopher Turner, audiology professor at the University of Iowa and a study investigator. They are far more able to follow and appreciate music.

Researchers expect to continue the trial through at least next year [2007] before going to the Food and Drug Administration for approval, says Aaron Parkinson, coordinator of clinical studies at Cochlear Corp. in Denver, which manufactures the device. By some estimates, a successful hybrid device could eventually reach a population up to twice the size of the current implant market, he says. In the U.S. today, about 25,000 people use a traditional cochlear implant.

Reconnecting with the World

Still, hybrid users need to devote time and energy to relearning how to hear, says Dawna Mills, an audiologist and clinical trials director at L.A.'s House Clinic, which is participating in the study. At first, human speech, full of new hisses and whistles, may not even be understandable. But with time and months of training, the brain seems to adapt to its new world of sound. "It's not normal hearing," Mills says, "but it becomes normal for them."

Virginia Baker, 50, of Simi Valley, California, says it did take effort to learn how to hear again. (Her high-frequency hearing had been declining for unknown reasons since age 19.) Still, that struggle was preferable to giving in to the social isolation that she had seen envelop her deaf grandmother.

Before surgery, Baker had quit her job substitute teaching in elementary schools because kids' squeaky voices started to fall outside her hearing range. "I was almost afraid to go out," she says. With a hybrid implant, however, she felt secure enough in her new listening skills to get a part-time job as an office manager and go back to college, where she is earning As in her accounting courses. "The hybrid," she says, "allows me to go out there with the rest of the world and be a part of it."

CHAPTER 2

Controversies Surrounding Deafness and Hearing Impairment

Deafness Is a Culture, Like Any Other

Michelle Jay

In the following viewpoint a writer who prefers to be known as "Michelle Jay" makes the case for recognition of the culture that has developed among deaf people. The culture centers around the formalization of American Sign Language, she says, an event that took place in the mid-1960s. Since then, an important distinction has grown between the term "deaf" with a lowercase "d" and the uppercase "Deaf," which refers to the culture. In Deaf culture, she writes, speech is disparaged and signing is the only valued mode of communication. Members of Deaf culture have different values and codes of behavior, she notes. For example, unlike the mainstream culture, Deaf culture approves of staring. It also rejects the notion that there are degrees of deafness. Instead, members of Deaf culture are encouraged to reject all attempts to mimic the hearing. Michelle Jay holds a bachelor's degree in Deaf Studies from California State University, Northridge, and writes about Deaf culture online.

Photo on previous page. Because of their unique form of communication via sign language deaf people often seem from a different culture. (Ken Lax/Photo Researchers, Inc.)

SOURCE: Michelle Jay, "Deafness Culture Unveiled," *Start American Sign Language*. Copyright © 2008. Reproduced by permission of the author. http://www.startasl.com.

In 1965, Deaf culture was first recognized as a real culture. That was only forty years ago. [Deaf scholars] William Stokoe, Carl Croneberg, and Dorothy Casterline were the ones who introduced Deaf culture to the world. They wrote the *Dictionary of American Sign Language* and included information about the thriving culture of the Deaf.

Before the *Dictionary of American Sign Language* was published, people involved in the medical field and deaf education only saw deaf people in terms of their deafness or hearing loss. They never would have thought that Deaf people had their own culture.

Carol Padden defines a culture as learned behaviors of a group of people who share a language, rules for behavior, traditions, and values. Deaf culture fits this definition just like every other culture in the world. They have a language, values, rules for behavior, and traditions.

American Sign Language [ASL] is the language of choice for the members of Deaf culture. If you are not fluent in American Sign Language, you are not part of Deaf culture. American Sign Language is a real language just like any other language. William Stokoe was the first to publish the truth about ASL—that it has its own structure, grammar, and syntax separate from English. ASL is a real language and is the natural language of the Deaf.

> **FAST FACT**
>
> William Stokoe, an English professor, is widely credited with establishing the independent legitimacy of American Sign Language.

Deaf Cultural Values

- American Sign Language is the most valued [language] in Deaf culture. Speech and spoken English do not compare to the natural language of the deaf. Even if a deaf person can read lips, comprehension is nowhere near that of ASL.
- The preservation of ASL is also a value in Deaf culture. Sign systems have been invented to try to help deaf children learn English. These systems include Signed English, Cued Speech, and Sign Supported Speech, to

name a few. These systems are not supported in Deaf culture and are not even languages. These systems have deprived deaf children of learning their true language and the ability to communicate naturally.

- Not speaking is a value in the culture of the deaf. Because speech is often forced on deaf children, it represents deprivation and confinement to a Deaf adult. If you are hearing, know ASL, and are around a Deaf friend, turning and speaking to someone else leaves the Deaf person out and is incredibly rude.
- Socializing is highly valued in the culture of the Deaf. When you are deaf, having a social life is very important because there are usually very few Deaf people in a community. In a hearing world, having Deaf friends is necessary for support. Before text messaging phones, Deaf people would only communicate with their deaf friends through letters or in person. Today, Deaf people still take advantage of the time they have with their Deaf friends. They will stay at a gathering for hours and leave very late. Long goodbyes are more than common.
- The members of Deaf culture also value the literature of their culture. These are stories and cultural values that are passed down through signed communication. Deaf culture also has its own art, stories, poetry, theatre, jokes, games, and books. These avenues teach about Deaf culture and Deaf pride.

Rules for Behavior

- It is not rude to stare in Deaf culture. Not staring is actually rude in this culture. When someone is signing to you, if you break eye contact, you are very rude.
- Facial expressions are required when you are signing. Some non-manual behaviors are part of ASL grammar.
- When you introduce yourself in Deaf culture, you use your full name. Deaf people also ask each other for information about where they're from (what city they

grew up in), what school they went to (what residential school they attended), etc. The Deaf community is very small, so they try to find these commonalities with each other early in their introductions.

Among deaf people "Deaf culture" refers to shared values, language, and behaviors, and is not distinguished by degrees of hearing loss. (© Dennis MacDonald/Alamy)

No Degrees of Deafness

Deaf people also label themselves in different ways. People in hearing culture tend to label deaf people by their hearing loss—hard of hearing, hearing impaired, etc. In hearing culture, being hard of hearing is seen as better than being deaf. These labels are viewed the exact opposite in Deaf culture. Deaf people call themselves one thing and one thing only when they are part of Deaf culture—Deaf. The term "Deaf" has nothing to do with the degree of hearing loss. Using the term "hard of hearing" is actually viewed negatively in Deaf culture. Using it makes it look like you think you're better than everyone else (because that's how it's viewed in hearing culture). Using the term "hearing impaired" insinuates that you think there is something wrong with deaf people and that they desire to be "fixed." This is actually the opposite of what members of the culture of the Deaf believe; they are Deaf and proud! The terms "deaf" ("little d") and "Deaf" ("big D") are also used and have much different meanings. "Little d" refers to someone who cannot hear while "big D" refers to someone who is part of Deaf culture and shares the language, values, behaviors, and traditions of that culture.

Deaf culture is a real culture just like any other.

Deafness Does Not Amount to a Separate Culture

James Joyner

In the following article political scientist James Joyner criticizes what he sees as fanaticism among proponents of so-called Deaf culture. Taking note of intransigent protests at Gallaudet University, a flagship institution of higher education for the deaf, Joyner attacks the resentment toward those who are "not deaf enough." The conflation of deafness with minority identity politics is bizarre and harmful, he says. Quoting from an editorial written by the incoming president of Gallaudet, who was the target of protesters' rage, Joyner observes that there are many degrees of deafness and many ways of responding to it. Some grow up lipreading and speaking, and some learn sign language. What especially outrages him is the view of some Deaf culture advocates that cures for deafness are bad. Joyner himself grew up with steadily worsening sight. He eventually had corrective surgery. He says that to forgo a cure for a sensory disability would be an absurd choice. Joyner holds a doctorate in political science from the University of Alabama. He is the founder of the online journal of politics and foreign affairs analysis *Outside the Beltway*.

SOURCE: James Joyner, "Gallaudet Protests and Deaf Culture," *Outside the Beltway*, October 14, 2006. Reproduced by permission of the author.

Alongstanding controversy at the nation's only college for deaf students reached its inevitable apex yesterday [October 13, 2006] as dozens of protesters at Gallaudet University were arrested.

At least two dozen people were arrested Friday night as students continued to block the entrance to the nation's only liberal arts university for the deaf and hearing-impaired in a protest over its incoming president. Hundreds of Gallaudet University students have blocked access to campus buildings since Wednesday, and the incoming president has refused to step aside. Classes were canceled for a third day Friday.

The school's outgoing president, I. King Jordan, said he regretted authorizing the arrests but felt he had no other choice. "Gallaudet University has exhausted all means of communication and negotiation with those who have disrupted the university's educational processes and held the campus hostage to their demands," he said in a statement.

A large group of students and some faculty members are demanding the resignation of Jane K. Fernandes, who was appointed in the spring to succeed Jordan in January [2007]. Fernandes has said some people do not consider her "deaf enough" to be president. She was born deaf but grew up speaking and did not learn American Sign Language, the preferred method of communicating at Gallaudet, until she was 23.

Resentment Toward Assimilators

The whole controversy has been quite bizarre. What has become quite clear is that there is a strong subculture among the deaf that is akin to what we often observe among minority ethnic groups. There seems to be a strong resentment of deaf or hard of hearing people who try to assimilate into mainstream society rather than adopting a separate medium of communication and a unique lifestyle.

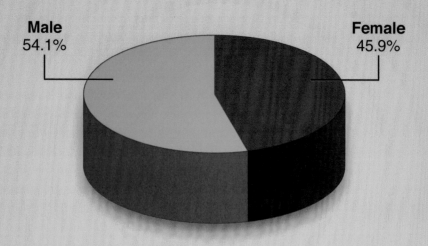

Deafness in Youth Is More Prevalent Among Males

Male 54.1%

Female 45.9%

Taken from: Gallaudet Research Institute, "Demographics," 2008.
http://gri.gallaudet.edu/Demographics/2008_National_Summary.pdf.

Fernandes wrote this in a [*Washington Post* opinion article] published in today's [October 14, 2006] edition:

> Our Gallaudet community is varied. There are many kinds of deaf people. Some are born to deaf parents; most are not. Some are lucky enough to grow up using American Sign Language. Others—like myself and increasing numbers of Gallaudet's students—learn and embrace ASL later in life. Some are deaf from birth; some become deaf later in life. Some benefit from the use of hearing aids or cochlear implants; others don't. Some have visual impairments or other disabilities.
>
> What unites all types of deaf people at our university is the rich history of the deaf community, American Sign Language and Deaf culture that has shaped Gallaudet's mission and character. As divided as we might seem right now, we are united in our commitment to that mission and character.

But what we see happening at Gallaudet is not just about being deaf. Just as there is diversity in ways of being deaf, the deaf community shares with the larger society diversity of age, gender, disability, racial and ethnic background, religion, sexual orientation and socioeconomic class. Just as in the larger society, racism exists within the deaf community. Deaf people of color face discrimination not only because of their hearing status (termed audism) but because of their race—even from within the deaf community. Deaf people of color and others from diverse groups must be included and are just as central to Gallaudet's mission and character as are our commitments to American Sign Language and Deaf culture. Currently, they are not.

During the presidential search and selection process, the issues of audism and racism that have plagued the deaf community for centuries came to the forefront. Long rumbling under the surface, they erupted like a volcano. I happened to be the person standing next to that volcano. The heat and fury of the eruption are the result of suppressed frustrations due to racism and audism, disagreements on how best to address them, and how best to preserve and support Deaf culture and American Sign Language in an age when deaf people are more diverse than ever.

There are those who would have us hunker down, fighting audism by excluding those who are not already like us. If Gallaudet took this approach, we would find ourselves shrinking to insignificance as the diversity of deaf, hard-of-hearing and deaf-blind people looked to other institutions to welcome them, however imperfectly. . . .

Perverse Opposition to Cures

Obviously, people with a given disability share common obstacles and experiences which will create some unity. Still, their forming such a strong subcultural identity is quite odd to me. Presumably, after all, the intermediate goal would be to do whatever is possible to overcome the disadvantages imposed by that disability in order to adapt to the world around them. Ultimately, one would hope that advances in medical science would cure the disability.

Yet, there is a strong sentiment among many of these groups that manifests in resisting the very idea of a "cure." Many handicapped people consider themselves merely "different" and view the idea that they should be "cured" much the way homosexuals do. For example, [*Superman* actor] Christopher Reeve was vilified by many for not simply accepting that he was confined to a wheelchair and instead undergoing aggressive treatments in a (futile, it turned out) attempt to regain the use of his limbs.

Gallaudet University president-designate Jane Fernandes speaks to the media and students by sign language during the October 2006 protests by students. (**AP Images**)

Because of heredity, my eyes became progressively unable to see instant objects starting around age 8. Rather than simply accepting that fact, my parents took me to an optometrist and bought me corrective lenses (Buddy Holly style eyeglasses). I went through perhaps twenty pairs of glasses over the next several years owing to ever-stronger prescriptions, breakage, and loss until getting contact lenses in my early twenties. About six years ago, I had corrective surgery (Lasik) that gave me "uncorrected" vision approximating 20/20. By that point, my uncorrected eyes had gotten to the point where I needed to put on eyeglasses to see my contact lenses so that I could get the first one ready for insertion. About two years ago, as I had been warned, I had early onset presbyopia, a side effect of the Lasik, and began needing very weak reading glasses to help me read small print or work long periods at the computer. Were there safe and reasonably affordable surgery available to give me perfect vision, I wouldn't hesitate an instant.

Granted, being nearsighted is orders of magnitude less debilitating than being deaf or quadriplegic. It's also sufficiently commonplace that, aside from confronting some stereotypes and being called "four eyes" as a kid, there's little social consequence. Still, I can't imagine that people would simply choose not to wear corrective lenses or that people with glasses would shun people who had Lasik surgery.

Deafness Is a Disability

Cathy Young

Students rarely have much to say about who is chosen as the president of their university. At Gallaudet University, however, a prolonged series of protests over the appointment of Jane K. Fernandes brought to wider attention the rift between those who regard deafness as something to be overcome and those who embrace it as a culture. In the following article journalist Cathy Young examines the controversy for signs that the protesters have gotten carried away by the notion of deafness as a source of identity politics. Acknowledging that the deaf have suffered unfair discrimination and worse, Young nevertheless argues that it is absurd to disregard the fact that deafness is a disability and, moreover, one that can be treated in many instances. She is especially concerned about deaf children who may be denied treatment so as to preserve their "Deaf" identity. Young is a contributing editor to the libertarian magazine *Reason* and a frequent columnist in the *Boston Globe*.

SOURCE: Cathy Young, "Radicalism in the Deaf Culture," *Boston Globe*, November 6, 2006. Copyright © 2006 Globe Newspaper Company. Reproduced by permission of the author.

S ince last May [2006], Gallaudet University, the world's only university designed entirely for deaf and hard-of-hearing students, has been rocked by protests over the selection of a new president.

Jane K. Fernandes was scheduled to take over from I. King Jordan in January. On Oct. 29 [2006], after protesters shut down the Washington campus for more than two weeks, the board of trustees revoked Fernandes's appointment. This fiasco is a striking example of identity politics gone mad.

In 1988, protesters rebelled against the appointment of a hearing president, Elisabeth Singer, and demanded a deaf president (something Gallaudet had never had since its founding in 1864). Singer resigned, and Jordan was appointed in her place.

"Not Deaf Enough"

Fernandes, the Gallaudet provost whom Jordan wanted to see as his replacement, is also deaf; but to some, "not deaf enough." She grew up lip-reading and speaking and learned sign language only as a graduate student.

In recent weeks, anti-Fernandes students and professors have denied that their objections had anything to do with her not being deaf enough, and have accused her of raising the issue to pose as a victim of political correctness. However, the *Washington Post* reports that the protesters backed off the "not deaf enough" complaint only when they realized that it wasn't likely to garner sympathy from the outside world. They focused instead on Fernandes's supposedly autocratic and intimidating leadership style and her alleged lack of interpersonal skills (one critic quoted by the Inside Higher Ed website even noted that she didn't smile enough).

There were also vague charges that she is insufficiently committed to fighting racism. Yet none of these

> **FAST FACT**
>
> In contrast to blind people, deaf people do not get a special break on federal taxes for their disability.

gripes seem sufficient to justify the passion that led to her ouster: the protests included hunger strikes and threats of violence.

An Exclusive View

Some of the criticisms publicly leveled at Fernandes are overtly rooted in identity politics. In a letter to the *Post*, Gallaudet English professor Kathleen M. Wood excoriated both Fernandes and Jordan for taking the position that Gallaudet is for all deaf students. This misguided inclusiveness, Wood asserted, had attracted deaf students who were "not integrating into Deaf culture" and resisting the use of sign language. She ended her letter by stating, "The new Gallaudet will not be for everyone."

"Deaf culture"—that's Deaf with a capital D—has flourished at Gallaudet. It is a radical movement that views deafness not as a disability but as an oppressed minority status akin to race, and also as a unique linguistic

The author is concerned that the protests at Gallaudet University were more about the Deaf culture movement as an oppressed minority than about real deaf culture. (**AP Images**)

The Culturally Deaf Are a Large Portion of Signers but a Small Portion of the Hearing Impaired

Estimates of number of:

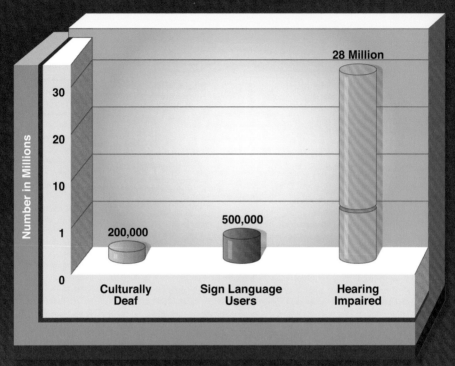

Taken from: MSN Encarta, "Deaf Culture," 2009. http://encarta.msn.com/encyclopedia_761595629/deaf_culture.html.

culture. The movement holds that there is nothing wrong with being deaf, only with how society has treated deaf people.

Few would deny that, historically, deaf people and others with disabilities have endured stereotyping, bias, and unfairness. Much progress has been made toward seeing people with disabilities as whole individuals, toward focusing on what they can do, not on what they can't. But it's a leap from this understanding to the bizarre idea that the lack of hearing is no more a disability than being female or black. (Verbal communication aside, surely being unable to hear environmental sounds often places a person at a serious disadvantage.)

The majority of deaf people do not belong to Deaf culture. It is estimated that at most a quarter of profoundly deaf people in the United States use sign language. Yet at many schools for the deaf, signing has been dogmatically treated as the only acceptable communication; children with some hearing have received little training in auditory and speaking skills. Deaf schools that promote "oralism" have been targeted for protests.

Deaf Deserve Cures

More harmful still, Deaf activists have railed against cochlear implants, which enable many deaf children to gain functional hearing; some deaf parents have denied implants to their children on ideological grounds. The activists also oppose research into cures for deafness through gene therapy and other means. To them, attempts to "fix" deafness amounts to nothing short of genocide.

Fernandes herself embraces Deaf culture, but she does not want it to be isolated from the hearing world or exclude those who don't meet purist standards of "Deafness." She also believes that the deaf community must deal honestly with the challenges posed by advances in medicine.

When this sensible view is rejected under pressure from a handful of radicals, it is a testament to the madness that can prevail when oppressed-minority status becomes a weapon to silence critics.

Deafness Should Not Be Treated as a Disability

Elaine Jarvik

For those with normal hearing, imagining the experience of the deaf can be hard. In the following article journalist Elaine Jarvik helps us understand the resentments and concerns that many deaf people harbor after decades of being treated as stupid and incapable of making decisions for themselves. She goes on to present the view that their deafness should not be regarded as a disability. Jarvik begins by relating some deaf humor showing how a disability can be turned into an advantage under some circumstances. The perception of some deaf people that they have been badly treated by mainstream society has led to the rise of what is known as Deaf culture, Jarvik explains. It comes complete with its own politics, contending for control of the educational decisions about deaf youth. Deaf culture leaders advocate American Sign Language as the main communication medium for deaf children. However, rapidly evolving technology, such as the cochlear implant, is complicating the choices policy makers and parents must make about the status of deafness as a disability or culture. Elaine Jarvik is a reporter for the Salt Lake City–based *Deseret News* who frequently writes about health issues.

SOURCE: Elaine Jarvik, "The (Deaf) Culture Wars," *Deseret News*, February 4, 2007. Copyright © 2007 The Deseret News Publishing Co. Reproduced by permission.

Ok, so there's this Deaf couple staying at a motel, and in the middle of the night the woman asks her husband to go buy her some aspirin. So he gets out of bed and drives to an all-night drugstore, and when he gets back the motel is dark and he can't remember which room is his. At first he doesn't know what to do, but then he drives to the middle of the parking lot and begins honking the horn. Pretty soon lights start going on in room after room, and people are peering out their windows to see who's making all that noise. The man waits until every room is lit up—and then drives to the one room that's still dark.

That's the famous motel joke, signs Minnie Mae Wilding-Diaz. She is sitting in her living room in Riverton [Utah] with her husband, Julio Diaz, who is also deaf. In the kitchen, her three deaf children are playing with Legos.

In Wilding-Diaz's motel joke, the tables have been turned. The Deaf man has used sound—and the hearing world's predictable attentiveness to it—to his advantage. In the joke, the hearing world has to accommodate.

In reality, says Wilding, it has been the hearing who have historically been in charge, the hearing who have decided what the rules are, what's normal and what's not. "Audism," some people call that. Or "phono-centric." Or even, sometimes, "colonialism."

The 16th Winter Deaflympics are in full swing in Salt Lake City this week [February 2007], which makes this a good time to see some elite skiing and hockey and also to explore what it means to be Deaf with a capital D. For people who can hear, that exploration sometimes feels like visiting a foreign country, across an ocean of silence and a cultural divide.

Denying Disability

To be Deaf with a capital D, says Julie Eldredge, a Deaf teacher of Deaf culture at BYU [Brigham Young University], is to believe first and foremost that deafness is not a disability or a pathology. Being deaf, she says, is just another way of being. There's nothing that needs fixing, and "hearing-impaired" is not a suitable synonym. Sound and speech aren't the goal; communication is.

"Deafness doesn't hurt, it doesn't kill you, it isn't a disease," says Julie's hearing husband, Bryan, who heads the American Sign Language and Deaf studies program at Utah Valley State College. "It's just a kind of existence. A perfectly acceptable existence. But hearing people have always been uneasy with people who aren't like them."

Not everybody who can't hear is culturally deaf, he says. People who grow old and lose their hearing may be deaf but they're not Deaf. Ditto for many people who grew up deaf but wore hearing aids or learned to lip read. Diane Larsen, who has been a lip reader since a bout of meningitis at age 4 and who now has a cochlear implant, says she has never considered herself culturally Deaf.

To be Deaf with a capital D means being part of a tight-knit community that values candidness and friendship and stretches across the United States and beyond. It also means being embroiled in culture wars about the education and future of deaf children and the future of Deaf culture itself.

Signing Is Central

Julio Diaz likes to tell this joke: A lumberjack goes into the forest to cut down a tree. He chops and chops, and when the tree is almost ready to fall he yells "Tim-ber!" But nothing happens. He chops a little bit more and yells "Tim-ber" again. Still nothing. So he goes to get a doctor, who comes back and examines the tree. Ah, says the doctor. The tree is Deaf. So the lumberjack *signs* "Timber!" in ASL. And the tree falls over.

American Sign Language, the joke suggests, is the best way to communicate with a Deaf tree or a Deaf person. That's Diaz's philosophy, too. Unlike his wife, who grew

Hearing Impairment Is Common, but Deafness Is Rare

Aged 15 years and older	Number of disabled in survey	Percent with specific characteristic
Used a wheelchair	2,707	1.2
Used a cane, crutches, or walker	9,144	4.1
Had difficulty seeing	7,868	3.5
Unable to see	1,806	0.8
Had difficulty hearing	7,830	3.5
Unable to hear	972	0.4

Taken from: U.S. Census. www.census.gov/hhes/www/disability/sipp/disab02/ds02ta.html.

up in a family with eight deaf siblings and two deaf parents, Diaz grew up in Puerto Rico in a family that never learned to sign. At the dinner table, he says, he would just eat and leave, since he felt left out of the family conversation. At school, where he was expected to lip read, "so many things in class flew by me. I would ask what something meant and they would tell me how to *say* it, but that's not what I was after."

Lip reading, says Deaflympics snowboarder Jeff Pollock, who teaches ASL at the University of Utah, is difficult when the teacher's back is turned. Only 30 percent of speech happens with the lips anyway, "and the rest is just a guesswork," says Pollock, who spent his school years having "no idea what was going on."

Few Hearing Parents Sign

It's a familiar story among Deaf adults who grew up in a strongly "oral" education system. Vealynn Jarvis, a Pleasant Grove hearing mother of a Deaf daughter who is now 35, remembers when Heather had her hands slapped for using ASL in school.

Like Diaz and Pollock, 90 percent of deaf children nationwide grow up in a hearing family. According to Annette Stewart, a clinical social worker at the Sanderson Community Center of the Deaf and Hard of Hearing in Taylorsville, 73 percent of those hearing parents don't learn to sign beyond superficial conversation. Pollock says he feels closer to his Deaf friends than to his family, who never learned to sign. Wilding-Diaz says many of the Deaf friends she grew up with in Idaho—friends whose families were hearing—didn't even know what their parents did for a living.

Not surprisingly, most of these hearing parents want their children to be like them, to grow up in a world full of sound and music and speech. Now, with the advent of more finely tuned digital hearing aids and cochlear implants, the stakes are even higher—and the rift between and in the Deaf culture is even more apparent, even though some in the Deaf community do now accept implants as "one option," Pollock says.

A recent study conducted by Utah State University's National Center for Hearing Assessment and Management found that 85 percent of parents with newly identified deaf children say they want their children to learn to speak and hear. "Parents want amplification (for their deaf children) at a year old or younger," says Rich Harward, director for the Newborn Hearing Screening Program for the Utah Department of Health. For most children that means hearing aids, or cochlear implants for children who can't benefit from hearing aids. Very few children, he says, "can't benefit from some sort of amplification," although no one touts the hearing aids or the implants as a "cure" for deafness. There are some children for whom hearing aids and implants don't work, especially well enough to understand speech.

FAST FACT

Deaf education was introduced to the United States in the mid-nineteenth century by Thomas Hopkins Gallaudet, whose work culminated in the founding of the Columbia Institute for the Deaf in 1864. It is now known as Gallaudet University.

Technology Changes Everything

Harward predicts that the new technologies will decrease the number of people who feel they are part of Deaf culture.

On a recent afternoon at Millcreek Elementary, speech tutor Chris Franco worked with 6-year-old Joshua Dyal, who wears a cochlear implant. Putting her hand over her mouth so he couldn't see her lips, Franco asked Joshua questions like "Where does a whale live?" and "Where do you keep your pillow?" Joshua responded clearly: "A whale lives in the ocean" and "I keep my pillow on my bed," although he struggled a bit with the "p" in "pillow."

Across the valley, on the same afternoon, a group of third-, fourth- and fifth-graders at the Jean Massieu School [JMS] in West Jordan were practicing signing "The Star Spangled Banner" for the Opening Ceremonies of the 16th Winter Deaflympics, raising their fists triumphantly on the word "brave." JMS, a charter school, is what is known as a bi-bi school for the Deaf: bilingual (ASL and English) and bicultural (Deaf and hearing); every teacher signs in ASL. The school was started by Wilding-Diaz and Diaz, who were frustrated that the Utah Schools for the Deaf and the Blind had no bi-bi option. There are now 55 students, preschool through 10th grade.

A school like this is the gold standard to someone like Dwight Benedict, chairman of the 16th Winter Deaflympics. A school where everyone signs provides a "critical mass" of children who can communicate with each other and learn from each other, and have access to Deaf adults in a way that some deaf children never do, he says.

(Some deaf children, says Bryan Eldredge, figure either they'll die before they become adults or will turn into a hearing person—since they've never really known a deaf adult. Wilding, an assistant professor at UVSC, says some deaf adults have been so unexposed to the kind of "incidental learning" that happens from communicating with their peers that when they get together with other deaf people, there are questions like "what is bank interest?" and "how do you buy a car?") . . .

Struggles over Language

Many school districts and schools for the deaf around the country have turned to strategies such as Manual Coded English and Signed Exact English, says Lawrence Fleischer, chairman of the Deaf studies department at California State University-Northridge and president of the USA Deaf Sports Federation. And that's a big mistake, he says. "It's an artificial language," Fleisher said. Whereas ASL has its own grammatical structure, MCE and SEE try to use English word order and English equivalents of words. "It doesn't work," he says.

Julie Eldredge gives this example: the word "outstanding." In ASL, there's a simple sign. But in MCE she would have to sign the word for "out" and then the word

Many school districts, such as Talladega County, Alabama, have begun teaching Manual Coded English (MCE) to deaf students instead of the more traditional American Sign language (ASL). **(AP Images)**

for "stand" and then "ing." That not only takes longer, she says, it's confusing.

"But who controls deaf education? Hearing people," says Fleischer. "They'll keep what they feel close to. I'm hoping for open dialogue about what's working. But we're powerless."

In some school districts in Utah, says Pollock, interpreters for deaf children have been told to use MCE instead of ASL. Pollock is vice president of a new group called the Henry C. White Educational Council, which wants a say in deaf education in the state. He says that deaf students don't graduate from Utah schools on par with hearing 12th-graders.

In his former job as coordinator of deaf services at the U., he says, he saw transcripts of deaf students who had gotten straight A's in high school but were entering college with junior-high-level English and math skills. Teachers' low expectations—"coddling" deaf students, Wilding-Diaz calls it—are only part of the problem, say Deaf advocates, who also point to the lack of qualified interpreters for students who need them. . . .

Emotional Challenges

With or without good interpreters, argues Pollock, some deaf students—particularly those in neighborhood schools in outlying areas where there may be only one or two deaf students—feel isolated and lonely. "This is also true of relationships with parents, siblings, family," he says. "It is much more common than anyone wants to admit."

And so it's no wonder that people who are deaf have more "mental health needs" than hearing people do, says social worker Stewart. Isolation is a big factor, especially for deaf individuals who grow up in families where there is little communication, she says. While it's estimated that in the hearing population 1 to 3 percent need some sort of mental health services, in the deaf population it's

15 to 54 percent, yet only 2 percent of those people get help, she says.

The big need is for therapists who sign, including deaf therapists. Even a good interpreter is only a next-best solution in such confidential exchanges, she says. "If a hearing person doesn't want to use an interpreter (in therapy), why would a deaf person?"

Even though there are 10 deaf social workers in the state, "no one is hiring them," and an attempt to get a state mental health coordinator position for the deaf has failed twice, she says.

But in many ways, this is a great time in history to be deaf. Technologies like the videophone are transforming the way deaf people can communicate with each other and with the hearing world.

Cochlear Implants Are Good for the Deaf

Shelley Neal

The use of cochlear implants has revolutionized the lives of parents raising deaf children. But is it good for the children themselves? In the following viewpoint Shelley Neal relates her own doubts as the mother of a young deaf child and then tells how those doubts were overwhelmingly resolved in favor of the technology. Her daughter Emily was born with little or no hearing in either ear, and instead of learning to speak she began to learn how to sign. While still a toddler, Emily became a candidate for cochlear implants. However, her mother had qualms about the ethics of sending a healthy, happy child into surgery to enable her to communicate with others orally, when sign language was available to those who wanted to make the effort to communicate with her. In the end, she approved the surgery, and the results have been so positive that she now has no regrets. The benefits of cochlear implants, she concludes, far surpass the hazards of implant surgery. Neal is a stay-at-home mother and student who lives in Chesapeake, Ohio.

SOURCE: Shelley Neal, "Cochlear Implants Let Children Live Life with Sound," *Herald-Dispatch*, February 25, 2009. Reproduced by permission of the author.

Cochlear implants deliver miraculous results to those who are profoundly deaf. Children who were once destined to live life in complete silence are now able to benefit from the advances made through modern technology. The cochlear implant is an excellent choice for parents who want their children to experience the world of sound.

As the mother of a child with bilateral cochlear implants, my experience began when my daughter, Emily, was diagnosed with profound hearing loss in both ears. While other babies were learning to use their voices to communicate, Emily was learning to use her hands. Living the first year of her life in silence, Emily was oblivious to sound. Since no one else in her family knew sign language, Emily's communication was limited to conversing with me, her mother.

During a visit with Dr. Thomas Jung, Emily's neurotologist, I learned that Emily was an excellent candidate for the cochlear implant. Upon hearing this, I became overjoyed, yet uneasy, being as no surgery comes without risks. Emily was a happy child and loved beyond words. Why would I purposely send her into surgery when she is already perfect? Why can't everyone just learn how to sign? These questions continually lingered in my mind, as I had a life-changing decision to make for my child. Nonetheless, a decision had to be made.

FAST FACT

Certain cochlear implants raise the risk of meningitis in children. However, the Food and Drug Administration says that the risk is slight and can be reduced through vaccination.

Rapid Progress

While spending time in prayer, I asked the Lord to use her for His glory and chose to go forward with the surgery. One month following surgery, Emily's cochlear implant was activated. Immediately after activation, her audiologist, Pamela Vannoy-Adkins, turned the device on; Emily cried in horror! She was experiencing a new sense: sound. Going from a peaceful environment to one filled with noise, simply overwhelmed her. Once again, I questioned my decision.

Prior to surgery, Emily was attending speech therapy at Marshall University twice a week to learn sign language. After receiving her cochlear implant, Emily's therapist, Amy Knell, focused on her oral communication skills. Emily was eager to learn and made every effort to understand the sounds around her and tried to make sense of them. Everyone marveled at her progress. After five years of intensive speech therapy and many prayers, Emily had reached her full potential and was discharged from the program. She has since undergone a second cochlear implant operation making her the first child in the state to acquire bilateral cochlear implants.

A young boy hears for the first time after receiving a cochlear implant. (**PHANIE/Photo Researchers, Inc.**)

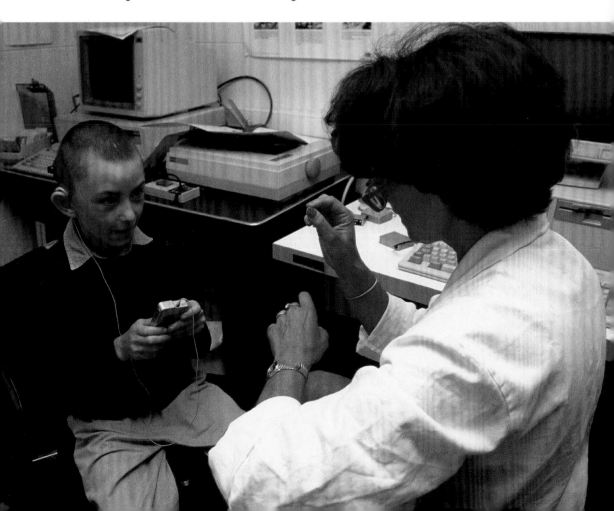

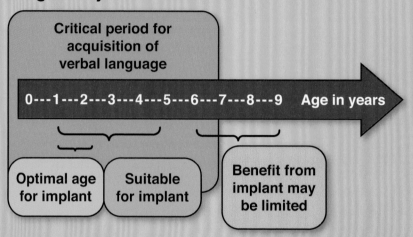

Early Implants Promote Oral Language Learning

Congenitally Deaf Children

Critical period for acquisition of verbal language

0---1---2---3---4---5---6---7---8---9   Age in years

Optimal age for implant

Suitable for implant

Benefit from implant may be limited

Taken from: National Cochlear Implant Users Associations, "Are Cochlear Implants Suitable for Children?" www.nciua.org.uk/Cochlear-Implants-for-Children.html.

Today, Emily is a first-grader who makes straight "A's," and reading is her favorite subject. Had I made a different decision, Emily would either be in a school for children with special needs or would require a sign language interpreter throughout her life. Watching her interact with her peers and hearing the words "I love you Mommy," validates the decision I made for her six years ago. The benefits of the cochlear implant far outweigh the risks. Thank God for Dr. Jung, the staff at Tri-State Otolaryngology, Amy Knell, the Scottish Rite Program at Marshall University and modern technology in the form of the cochlear implant.

Cochlear Implants Are Bad for the Deaf

Matthew S. Moore, interviewed by Jessica Young

The idea of refusing to accept technology that can restore hearing to the deaf might strike some people as strange. In the following viewpoint, however, deaf publisher Matthew S. Moore argues that to some deaf people there are more downsides than advantages to the cochlear implant. Some deaf people are put off by reports of terrible experiences that some who have undergone the surgery have suffered. Others, he says, have no problem with the implants but still choose not to make use of them. Their life experience has made them comfortable with being deaf, and they do not want to change. Underlying the issue, he argues, is the history of disrespect that deaf people have had to endure. Being treated as feeble-minded and helpless has left them embittered. So, for many, the cochlear implant is a threat to the gain in self-respect that deaf people have achieved through the spread of sign language. It is the invention of sign language that differentiates the deaf from all other disabled, he claims. Moore is the publisher of *Deaf Life* magazine, and he operates several Web sites, including CochlearWar.com.

SOURCE: Jessica Young, "Con: One Opponent's View on Cochlear Implants," Suburban Life Publications (mysuburbanlife.com), January 6, 2009. Reproduced by permission.

[Jessica Young] *Q: What are some of the deaf community's concerns over cochlear implants?*

[Matthew S. Moore] A: I know of persons who have had bad to horrendous experiences with their implants and others whose implants functioned well mechanically but who stopped using them. Mass-media coverage seems to prefer to focus on the glorious successes instead of the disturbing failures. Yet the indifferent results and the failures may outnumber the successes. I'm still not convinced of the long-term safety of implants. Many of my deaf friends shudder at the thought of getting implants. To us, it constitutes (an unnecessary) surgical invasion of our heads.

As for the social-cultural aspect, we're concerned about possible language deprivation. Typically parents are encouraged not to sign with their children or let their children sign, but instead to enroll them in an auditory-oral or auditory-verbal program. Auditory-verbal therapy bans all visual cues including speech reading and sign language, training the child to receive information through the auditory channel alone via amplification or implant. To us, this is an unnatural, grueling way to give deaf children basic language skills, as it forces them to rely exclusively on their weakest sensory channel. Deaf children are visual learners.

One major concern of ours is language rights. There are two contradictory trends: hearing parents signing with their hearing babies, encouraged by research that shows that early exposure to signing aids cognitive development; AND the trend for parents to approve bilateral implants for their deaf babies and then ensuring that they have no exposure to sign language. The deaf community's position is that all deaf children have a right to learn and use sign language freely, as it enriches their lives and gives them a strong foundation in the acquisition of language skills.

There is no way to predict how well a deaf child is going to function with implants. Implants do not provide a functionally equivalent sense of hearing. Children with implants still need speech therapy and elaborate technical and educational support. All too often, the child ends up with a debilitating language gap—substandard literacy and poor speech.

A History of Disrespect

Q: Many in the deaf community are offended by society's tendency to frame their lack of hearing as a "disability" that needs to be fixed and prefer to celebrate deafness as a culture, of sorts. Do you agree?

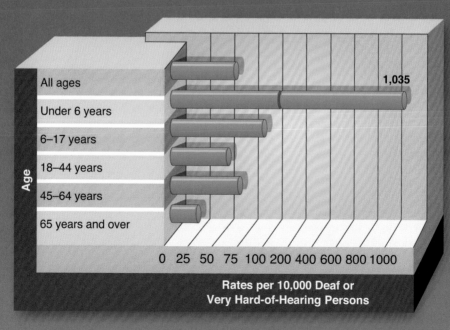

Cochlear Implants Are Mainly Performed on the Young

Taken from: National Institute on Deafness and Other Communication Disorders.
www.nidcd.nih.gov/health/statistics/implants.

A: Medically speaking, deafness is a disability—just as cerebral palsy and blindness are disabilities. However, unlike those with other disabilities, deaf people have created a rich and complex language—American Sign Language in this country. Culturally deaf people tend to see themselves as a quasi-ethnic or linguistic minority.

To properly understand why deaf people feel the way they do about cochlear implants—the latest in a long, long line of attempts to "fix" and "cure" deafness—you must understand history. The paternalism of oralists and the long-standing pathological views of deaf people that can still be found in the medical profession—seeing deaf people as less smart, less capable than hearing persons and seeing sign language as an inferior means of communication. The linkage of "deaf" with low expectations is still a problem that we grapple with every day.

Q: What is your response to implant proponents who say that deafness is a medical abnormality and that every

The downside of cochlear transplants is that they can be frightening to some deaf children because they get overwhelmed with all the new sounds and often require speech therapy. (© **Picture Partners/Alamy**)

effort should be made to rectify it in order to allow someone to achieve a higher level of functionality both in terms of academics, social life and general bodily safety?

A: I would agree wholeheartedly with this sentiment—had deaf people not invented sign language as a means to communicate.

I'd have to say that most deaf people resent the implication that they're abnormal (or) defective in any way. They'd say, "What do you mean abnormal? I have a job; I work; I drive; I vote; I pay taxes; I go shopping; I enjoy gardening and shooting baskets." We see ourselves not as defective auditory specimens but as whole, normal persons. We communicate differently, and our communicative needs are different from those of hearing people. But we're normal.

> **FAST FACT**
>
> Cochlear implant surgery carries risks. Among them are facial paralysis, meningitis, tinnitus, and damage to the sensation of taste, according to the Food and Drug Administration.

A Question of Empowerment

The insidious implication of the pathological view is that, unless we get surgically altered and install costly biotechnological devices, we're abnormal? Is that what it means? So only deaf persons with implants are normal?

As for academics, mainstreaming has had a devastating impact on our community, and why? Many deaf children do not thrive in that kind of environment. Many are alienated and adrift. Many don't get access to the same information as their hearing classmates. Tossing in an interpreter and notetaker doesn't create educational parity.

The cochlear-implant controversy embodies a question of empowerment: Do we control our own destinies, or do hearing persons—whether they are our parents, audiologists or surgeons—make those decisions for us?

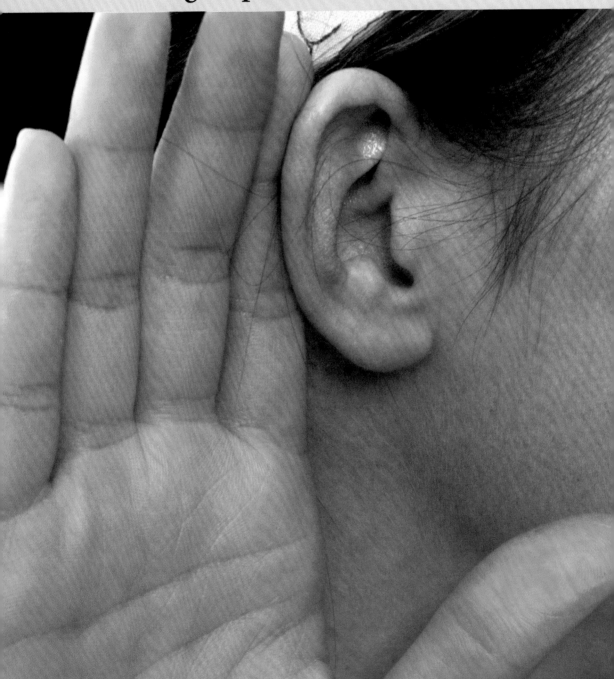

CHAPTER 3

Personal Experiences of Deafness and Hearing Impairment

The Sounds of Silence

Judy Metter

The onset of hearing loss varies widely. In the following article Judy Metter relates the saga of her loss over decades. Parties were the first problem, she says. She had trouble making out what people were saying when the background chatter got in the way. The doctor told her she had a mild case of nerve damage in her ear. However, the situation worsened. She realized that sounds she had routinely heard before were no longer audible. With a hearing aid she got some relief, but even that was transient. Moreover, she had to cope with the embarrassment of being a woman in her thirties wearing a hearing aid. Eventually, she learned that she had a hereditary condition that leads to gradual but progressively worse hearing loss. Even while accepting the diagnosis, she remains determined to hang onto hope. Judy Metter lives in Los Angeles and is an office manager for an international film production company.

SOURCE: Judy Metter, "Work in Progress," HearingLoss.org, July 13, 2004. Reprinted with permission from *Hearing Loss Magazine*. Copyright 2004 Hearing Loss Association of America. www.hearing loss.org.

Photo on facing page. Whether because of genetics or accident the loss of hearing is a traumatic event. (© avatra images/Alamy)

If you want to read a story with a happy ending, turn the page, because this story is still in the telling. The goal is a happy ending but sometimes, for some people, at certain points in their life, reading about the struggle is easier to relate to than the happy ending.

My story began when I was in my twenties. I'd always had great hearing. Every Sunday morning I would complain to my downstairs neighbors when their children would wake me up with their ruckus, the sounds of their playing and laughter, and their balls bouncing against the walls. These sounds drove me to distraction. Be quiet! Let me sleep! Oh, if only I knew then what I know now.

The beginning of my hearing loss was gradual. I started having trouble hearing people at parties. But only at parties. I could still be awakened on Sunday morning by the children. After a series of "problem parties," I went to an ear doctor thinking maybe I had wax that needed to be removed. Not the case. I was diagnosed with mild inner-ear nerve damage (as in too much rock and roll music).

Hearing aids wouldn't help that condition, the doctor said. The advice was to pay more attention to the person with whom I was speaking at the party. This would make that person feel very special because I would appear to be so intensely interested in what he or she was saying while giving me the chance to focus on their words.

I could still hear at dinner parties, could still hear on the phone, movies, TV, plays, radios records, "through walls." So, I didn't give it a third thought.

Signs of Growing Loss

But, then came walls—literally. I suddenly discovered I couldn't hear through them any more. My boss never missed a chance to mention to me that he thought I had a hearing problem. I never missed a chance to remind him he already knew that. I worked out a system, though. Every time he would yell to me from his office, I would pick up the phone, call him on the intercom and say, "What?" It worked for a while.

But, then came the accents. In my mid-thirties, I changed jobs and went to work for an English company. Both my bosses had thick accents. I discovered it's harder to read the lips of someone with an accent. Oh well.

Now, this was about the time that President [Ronald] Reagan was fitted with hearing aids. After a friend showed me an article about him and the House Ear Institute, I figured that is where I should go. If they were good enough for the President of the United States, they certainly would be good enough for me. I made an appointment immediately.

On my first visit, I was tested and my audiologist said, with a big smile, "Of course, hearing aids will help!" I said, with tears in my voice "Great, fit me up."

Feeling Awkward

I have to admit the hearing aids helped but I felt like a freak. I was embarrassed for anyone to see them—after all, I was still relatively young and hearing aids were either for elderly people, which I wasn't, or people with disabilities, which I wouldn't face. And, on top of that, I was single. Who would want me now?

Okay, no parties, no walls, no accents, but I still had the phone, movies, TV, plays, radios, records. Until my boss asked me to write down the lyrics from a record. Does 75 percent count? Scratch the records.

But, I still had the phone, movies, TV, plays, and the radio.

My hearing at that point seemed to stabilize, and I became accustomed to putting my hearing aids in every day, became more comfortable showing them to people, and learned to tell people straight away that I was hard of hearing, to please look at me when they spoke. Most people were polite or curious and saw that my willingness to talk about it made it easy for them to ask questions. I almost started to enjoy educating people on the plight of people with hearing loss. Even the men I'd meet didn't seem to have a problem with it.

Support Group

In my early forties, I started having trouble with movies (oh no, not movies!). I was in the film business and I loved, loved, LOVED movies. By this time, I had joined my local SHHH Chapter, which was probably the best thing I ever did. At these meetings, I would be surrounded by people who could relate to me and my problems. And at these meetings, I learned about speechreading classes, assistive listening devices, captioning, amplified phones, the ADA [Americans with Disabilities Act], etc. And, *I made friends.*

With the support of my group, I got up the nerve to ask for the headsets when I went to the movies. At first, very discreetly. I would hide them in my purse until I was seated in the dark of the theater. But, as I got used to them, and bolder about exposing my disability, I would ask for them in a strong voice and made sure people around me saw them. I discovered people were curious, would ask about them, and then would mention they had an aunt, mother, brother, friend who was hard of hearing and they couldn't wait to give them the news!

Now I'm in my early fifties. My television is captioned, my phone is amplified, no more plays (I go to dance performances or to hear orchestras), no records with lyrics (of course now they're CDs—I'm really dating myself!), radio only in the car, and captioned videos. I only go to foreign films now because my speech discrimination has gotten so bad, the headsets don't work for me anymore. I ration parties because of the stress, arrange to go out with no more than two other people whenever possible, choose restaurants with care, and wear powerful behind-the-ear hearing aids. I'm able to do my job but it is very stressful, even with the caring people I work for. And, I wonder . . . what's next?

Challenges Continue

I have cochlear otosclerosis, a hereditary condition (my sister also has a hearing loss) for which, at this point, there is no cure, and surgery won't help. There's no telling where the deterioration will end. Will I become totally deaf? Will a cochlear implant work for me when the time comes? How will I continue to support myself? I'm dealing with loss of identity, loss of self-esteem, and I'm fighting depression.

Fortunately, I belong to a support group made up of wonderful women, professionals who happen to be hard of hearing. I see a therapist through the Deaf Program at St. John's Hospital in Santa Monica, California. And, I have great friends and family who go out of their way to try and understand what I'm going through and to help as much as possible.

I feel I have educated many, many people on the complexities of hearing loss, and they are amazed at how it can impact on a person's life. I explain what sound is like with hearing aids (try wearing a Walkman at high volume with three different radio stations playing at the same time). I explain how I can only hear about eight out of fifteen words in a sentence, how I can't tell the direction a sound is coming from, how I can hear *his* voice clearly but can't make out a word *she's* saying, and on and on. And, of course, the conversations where I might be talking about electric *cars* not realizing that everyone else is talking about electric *guitars*. Thank God I have a sense of humor!

So, I'm not at my happy ending yet. Since my hearing loss is degenerative, as soon as I get comfortable with the stage I'm in, I lose more hearing. I have something you might call a chronic adjustment syndrome. I am grieving the loss of the old me. I miss the old me. I still have to figure out a career shift, find my identity, get

> **FAST FACT**
>
> Otosclerosis is the most common form of hereditary hearing impairment. It typically strikes young adults, and 90 percent of affected persons are under fifty years of age at the time of diagnosis.

my self-esteem back, and completely accept rather than fight the changes.

I am not giving up though. I have a lot of work ahead of me, and I feel certain there is a light at the end of the tunnel. But, oh what I wouldn't give to be awakened on my Sunday mornings by the sounds of children laughing, screaming and bouncing balls against the walls. Oh yeah, and the garbage trucks at 6 A.M. That would be music to my ears!

Growing Up with Deaf Parents

Myron Uhlberg

In the following selection Myron Uhlberg presents a warm and loving portrait of his early childhood in a home with deaf parents. Uhlberg was born during the Great Depression, when even people with no disabilities were having trouble finding jobs. It was especially hard for deaf people, in an era that accorded them no rights and little respect, to make an independent living. Yet, Uhlberg's parents did. He recalls how they negotiated a lease on their apartment, dealt with their own less-than-supportive relatives, and earned a place for themselves in society. Uhlberg, who despite his relatives' doubts grew up hearing just fine, is an award-winning author of a number of children's books in addition to this memoir. He lives with his wife in Santa Monica and Palm Springs, California.

My first language was sign.

I was born shortly after midnight, July 1, 1933, my parents' first child. Thus I had one tiny reluctant foot in the first half of that historically fateful year,

SOURCE: Myron Uhlberg, *Hands of My Father: A Hearing Boy, His Deaf Parents, and the Language of Love.* New York, NY: Bantam Books, 2009. Copyright © 2009 by Myron Uhlberg. Used by permission of Bantam Books, a division of Random House, Inc.

and the other firmly planted in the second half. In a way my birth date, squarely astride the calendar year, was a metaphor for my subsequent life, one foot always being dragged back to the deaf world, the silent world of my father and of my mother, from whose womb I had just emerged, and the other trying to stride forward into the greater world of the hearing, to escape into the world destined to be my own.

Many years later I realized what a great expression of optimism it was for my father and mother, two deaf people, to decide to have a child at the absolute bottom of the Great Depression.

We lived in Brooklyn, near Coney Island, where on certain summer days, when the wind was blowing just right and our kitchen window was open and the shade drawn up on its roller, I could smell the briny odor of the ocean, layered with just the barest hint of mustard and grilled hot dogs (although that could have been my imagination).

Our apartment was four rooms on the third floor of a new red-brick building encrusted with bright orange fire escapes, which my father and mother had found by walking the neighborhood, and then negotiated for with the impatient hearing landlord all by themselves despite their respective parents' objections that they "could not manage alone" as they were "deaf and handicapped" and "helpless" and would surely "be cheated." They had just returned from their honeymoon, spent blissfully in Washington, D.C., planned to coincide with the silent, colorful explosion of the blossoming cherry trees, which my mother considered a propitious omen for the successful marriage of two deaf people.

Apartment 3A was the only home my father ever knew as a married man. Its four rooms were the place he lived with and loved his deaf wife, and raised his two hearing sons, and then left by ambulance one day forty-four years after arriving there, never to return.

Illness Took Dad's Hearing

One day my father's hands signed in sorrow and regret the story of how he had become deaf. This was a story he had pieced together from facts he had learned later in life from his younger sister, Rose, who in turn had heard it from their mother. (The fact that he had to learn the details of his own deafness from his younger hearing sister was a source of enduring resentment.)

My father told me he had been born in 1902, a normal hearing child, but at an early age had contracted spinal meningitis. His parents, David and Rebecca, newly arrived in America from Russia, living in an apartment in the Bronx, thought their baby would die.

My father's fever ravaged his little body for over a week. Cold baths during the day and wet sheet-shrouded nights kept him alive. When his fever at last abated, he was deaf. My father would never again hear a sound in all the remaining years of his life. As an adult, he often questioned why it was that he had been singled out as the only member of his family to become deaf.

I, his hearing son, watched his hands sign his anguish: *"Not fair!"*

My father and his father could barely communicate with each other. Their entire shared vocabulary consisted of a few mimed signs: *eat, be quiet, sleep.* These were all command signs. They had no sign for love between them, and his father died without ever having had a single meaningful conversation with his firstborn child.

My father's mother did have a sign for *love.* It was a homemade sign, and she would use it often. My father told me that his language with his mother was poor in quantity but rich in content. She communicated less through agreed-upon signs than through the luminosity that appeared in her eyes whenever she looked at him. That look was special and reserved for him alone.

Like their parents, my father's siblings—his younger brother, Leon, and his two younger sisters, Rose and

Millie—never learned a word of formal sign. They remained strangers to him his entire life. . . .

Sent Away to School

In 1910, when he was eight years old, my father's parents sent him to live at the Fanwood School for the Deaf, a military-style school for deaf children. My father thought they had abandoned him because he was damaged. In his early days there he cried himself to sleep every night. But ever so slowly he came to realize that rather than having been abandoned, he had been rescued. For the first time in his life he was surrounded by children just like him, and he finally understood that he was not alone in this world.

However, the education he received at Fanwood was certainly a mixed blessing. There, as at most deaf schools at the time, deaf children were taught mainly by hearing teachers, whose goal was to teach them oral speech. The deaf are not mute; they have vocal cords and can speak. But since they cannot monitor the sound of their voice, teaching them intelligible speech is extraordinarily difficult. Although my father and his classmates tried to cooperate with their teachers, not one of them ever learned to speak well enough to be understood by the average hearing person.

While this futile and much-resented pedagogic exercise was being inflicted on the deaf children, sign language was strictly forbidden. The hearing teachers considered it to be a primitive method of communication suitable only for the unintelligent.

Learning to Sign

Not until the 1960s would linguists decree ASL (American Sign Language) to be a legitimate language all its own. But long before then the deaf, among them the children at my father's school, had come to that conclusion themselves. Every night, in the dormitory at Fanwood, the older deaf children taught the younger ones the visual language of sign.

With sign, the boundaries of my father's silent mental universe disappeared, and in the resulting opening sign after new sign accumulated, expanding the closed space within his mind until it filled to bursting with joyous understanding.

"When I was a boy, I was sent to deaf school. I had no real signs," my father signed to me, his hands moving, remembering. "I had only made-up home signs. These were like shadows on a wall. They had no real meaning. In deaf school I was hungry for sign. All were new for me. Sign was the food that fed me. Food for the eye. Food for the mind. I swallowed each new sign to make it mine."

My father's need to communicate was insatiable and would cease only when the dormitory lights were turned out at night. Even then, my father told me, he would sign himself to sleep. Once asleep, my father claimed, he would dream in sign.

> **FAST FACT**
>
> The dominance of oral education for the deaf until recently owes much to the influence of German educator Samuel Heinicke, who spread his ideas about educating the deaf through articles widely published from 1773 to 1775.

Learning a Trade

My father was taught the printing trade in deaf school, an ideal trade, it was thought, for a deaf man, as printing was a painfully loud business. The unspoken message transmitted to the deaf children of that time by their hearing teachers was that they were neither as smart nor as capable as hearing children. Thus they would primarily be taught manual skills, like printing, shoe repair, and house painting.

Upon graduation in 1920, my father was able to land his first job, the job that would last his working lifetime.

"In the Great Depression," he told me, "I was lucky to have an apprentice job with the *New York Daily News*.

The author's father was sent to a school for the deaf in 1910. At the time schools for the deaf taught students oral speech, which hampered their ability to communicate because they could not monitor their own sounds and consequently did not speak well. (Topical Press Agency/Hulton Archive/Getty Images)

I knew it was because I was deaf and so wouldn't be distracted by the noise of the printing presses, and the clattering of the linotype machines, but I didn't care. I also didn't care that the deaf workers were paid less than the hearing workers because Captain Patterson, the big boss, knew that we wouldn't, couldn't, complain. He knew that we would be happy for any job, at any wage. We were deaf. He could hear. And he was right. The hearing people ran the world.

Proud to Earn Wages

"But those were tough times for me. By the time I gave my mother money out of my small pay envelope at the end of the week, for my room and board, and then some more for the household expenses, there was not much left over. My hearing brother and sisters did not have steady work. My mother and father were the janitors of our building, so they had little ready cash. It broke my heart to see my mother on her hands and knees, shuffling up and down the hallways, washing the wooden floors with hot, soapy water she dragged along behind her in a big wooden bucket. Her hands were always red and raw. To this day I can't get the memory of her chafed hands out of my mind. When I finally got my union card and made good union wages, I could give her enough money every month so she didn't have to do that anymore. You can't imagine how proud I was that I, her deaf son, could do that for her." . . .

My father's memories were so intense, and so tightly woven together in his mind, that in the midst of telling one story, he would often wander off into another one that rose to the surface almost as if it had been bottled up all these years and, now that there was someone to tell it to, had just worked itself free. When he did so, he would catch himself and terminate the beginning of the new memory by abruptly signing *another story*. And then I knew that, somewhere down the road, I would hear from him this *other story*.

Noisy Relatives

"On Sundays my mother, father, brother, and two sisters came down from the Bronx. They did not trust Mother Sarah's family. They brought their own pots and pans. Each one held a pot or a pan on their lap during the two-hour, three-subway-ride trip from way up in the Bronx to Kings Highway in Brooklyn. They practiced banging on the pots and pans while the subway cars went careening through the tunnels. The train's wheels made such a screeching sound that people on the car barely noticed them. When they got off the subway, my sisters and brother marched to our apartment house, still banging the pots and pans. They looked like some ragtag army in a Revolutionary War painting. As soon as they arrived at our apartment, they hid behind the head of your bed and pounded away, while they stomped their feet like a marching band. I felt the loud noise through the soles of my feet. They had a nice rhythm. The result was the same: you awoke immediately. Jumped, actually."

"This went on for a whole *year*?" I asked.

"Yes. They thought your hearing might go away. Just as hearing for me and Mother Sarah went away when we were young. Big mystery."

"How about our neighbors? All that banging and stomping, didn't they mind?" I asked.

"What do you expect?" my father answered. "We had to know if your hearing stayed with you. The neighbors threatened to call the landlord. Have us evicted. Mother Sarah sweet-talked them out of it. The notes flew fast and furious between them till they settled down. Anyway, they thought you were a cute baby. They also wondered if you could hear. They wondered if the deaf can have a hearing baby. We were the only deaf people they knew. They had no idea of our deaf ways."

Thinking for a minute, his hands added, striking each other sharply, "It was *hard* for Mother Sarah and me to figure out how to take care of you. But we did. We learned how to tell when you cried at night. You slept in your crib next to our bed when we brought you home from the hospital. We kept a small light on all night. Mother Sarah wore a ribbon attached to her wrist and to your sweet baby foot. When you moved your foot, she would immediately awaken to see the reason why. She still has that ribbon somewhere. Sign was your first language. The first sign you learned was *I love you*.

"That is a good sign. The best sign."

Coping with the Loss of Both Sight and Hearing

Rebecca Alexander

In the following article social worker Rebecca Alexander tells the moving story of her discovery that she suffers from Usher syndrome, a genetic disease that afflicts both hearing and sight. Alexander says she began having vision problems in sixth grade, but this is not especially unusual, so it did not fret her. At the time, she could not really understand that her poor sight was caused by retinitis pigmentosa, a gradual loss of cells in the retina, the patch at the back of the eye that converts light into electrochemical signals to the brain. As a young teen, she also began to lose some hearing. Still, it was not until she reached the age of nineteen that she got the bad news from a doctor: As an Usher syndrome patient, she was going to go blind and deaf before very long. Less than ten years later, the curtains are descending on her key senses. Sensing that she has little time left in the light-and-sound-filled world, she plans to make the most of every moment. Alexander holds master's degrees in public health and social work from Columbia University. She is considering starting a family but wants to be sure she will not pass on her syndrome to her children.

SOURCE: Anna Jane Grossman, "Out of Sight, Out of Sound," *Marie Claire*, November 2007. Reproduced by permission.

There are some things in life you know will happen, but they don't seem real. When you're a kid, you know you'll grow up, but you cannot imagine what it will feel like. You know you'll eventually die, but you don't spend every moment thinking about it.

That's how I felt nine years ago, at 19, when a doctor told me I was going to be both deaf and blind one day. I was scared, of course, but when you've always seen and heard, you can't comprehend life any other way. Only in the past year have I begun to understand what complete silence and darkness could be like.

The problems started in sixth grade, when I couldn't see the chalkboard. I went to several ophthalmologists where I sat completely still through long tests with wires attached to my eyeballs. I kept thinking, all this just to get glasses? Eventually, the doctors determined I had retinitis pigmentosa, an inherited disorder where the cells in the retinas slowly degenerate. They told my parents I'd be blind by the time I was an adult.

The diagnosis came as my parents were separating, and a new disagreement between them arose: how to break the news to me. They compromised, telling me I'd have difficulty seeing at night. But when you're 12, what does that mean? The whole thing didn't seem like a big deal to me.

A year later, my mom noticed that when she called me and my twin brother from downstairs, he'd answer but I wouldn't. The doctor just said, "No 13-year-old girl responds when her mother calls her."

Feeling Substandard

Then tests confirmed my hearing was getting worse, too.

In a weird way, it made sense to me that things were wrong. I could already tell I wasn't like my mother. She was flawless—even her singing voice and handwriting were perfect. I was sloppy. I lied. The diagnosis felt like proof of my inadequacy.

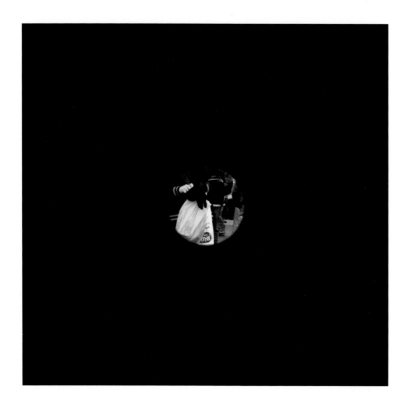

Rebecca suffers from Usher syndrome, which includes retinitis pigmentosa, a gradual deterioration of the retina that leads to tunnel vision. (Cordelia Molloy/ Photo Researchers, Inc.)

My family puts a lot of emphasis on being attractive. My mother taught us to be impeccably groomed at all times and well mannered, like mini newscasters—which, surprise, is exactly what my older brother grew up to be. But I didn't understand how I was supposed to be attractive *and* disabled.

As for my difficulties seeing, I was fine in small groups, like at home, where my brothers didn't treat me differently. But by the time high school hit, it was hard to decipher what I was and wasn't hearing and seeing, since I still thought I was catching everything. In reality, I was missing a lot; my teachers were always accusing me of daydreaming.

I got my first hearing aids in high school, but I would only wear them with my hair down, and only in history class because the teacher mumbled. At least I had the built-in coolness that came with being a twin. I was good at sports (so long as it wasn't a game with a small ball—those were becoming hard to see). And yet, I was starting to feel I didn't quite belong.

A Drunken Fall

One thing I did to fit in was drink. Usually, I only drank beer—and not an abnormal amount for a kid that age. But one night, a month before I was supposed to start at the University of Michigan, I sat in a playground with my twin brother, our friends, and a bottle of vodka. I got so drunk that my brother had to carry me home. Trying to walk to the bathroom in the middle of the night, I went out the bedroom window instead and fell 27 feet to the stone patio below.

It's hard to say if the alcohol or my eyesight caused the fall. I broke nearly everything and was in a wheelchair for months. The doctors were amazed I'd survived—although they seemed certain I'd never walk normally again. I did four months of nonstop physical therapy.

Around the time I went to Michigan a year later, my hearing took its first big dip. My family learned to whistle to get my attention. Still, I was resistant to wearing the aids, despite needing them more and more.

On dates, I was terrified of guys finding out I had disabilities. If I was with one who didn't know I had hearing aids, I'd slip them out while we were kissing and put them under the bed.

Worse yet, I started getting "doughnut vision," which meant I could see peripherally and straight ahead but not in the doughnut area in between.

When I started college, I understood I'd eventually lose my eyesight, but I thought my hearing would remain fairly stable. Then an otolaryngologist diagnosed me with Usher Syndrome, a genetic condition that affects about 20,000 people in the U.S. It causes people to

> **FAST FACT**
>
> There is no cure at present for Usher syndrome. However, some ophthalmologists believe that a high dose of vitamin A may slow, but not halt, the progression of vision loss that is part of the syndrome.

go both blind and deaf, either at birth or progressively. I hadn't considered that my vision and hearing losses were related and that I could—and would—lose both entirely.

Living with Usher Syndrome

Maybe I was seeking control in a chaotic situation, but soon I was wrestling with anorexia and exercise bulimia. I'd work out four to six hours a day until I went into rehab for a month after graduation. At least I was just as compulsive about my schoolwork: I asked other people to take notes for me. In one class, a girl had live closed-captioning at her desk; I read over her shoulder. I did well, graduating with honors.

I learned sign language and was surprised I enjoyed it. If you don't know how to do it, you almost feel like you're missing out when you watch people sign to each other. After graduating from Michigan, I went to Columbia University for two master's degrees in public health and clinical social work. Now I'm a social worker at a school for the deaf, and I organize seminars at the Foundation Fighting Blindness. I'm also developing a private practice as a psychotherapist treating eating disorders.

Still, Usher is a difficult subject to bring up, especially on a first date, although most of my boyfriends have been supportive. I recently dated someone who kept a cup by the side of his bed for my hearing aids. My last boyfriend let me teach him sign language, and we'd use it all the time for fun. It was our own private thing. . . .

Getting Things Done Now

Sometimes, my brain tries to compensate for lost peripheral vision by creating images. For a while, I kept a frying pan by my desk because when I was at my computer, I would think I saw a man walking by the door out of the corner of my eye. No one was there. I used to love going to the movies, but it's tiring since I'm constantly scanning my environment. Still, I teach eight Spinning classes a week—they're often in the dark, and I've memorized the layout of each Spin room. I think my students would be surprised to find out the person telling them to pedal harder can barely hear or see them.

I feel an urgency to do as much as possible while I can still see and hear somewhat. I want to travel—lately, to Zanzibar and Mauritius and Tibet. And I want to have a family. I'm torn between wanting to settle down before my condition gets worse—it's like having another clock ticking besides the reproductive one—and feeling too young and uncertain. There are issues with having kids. Usher is inherited, and if I marry someone who carries the gene, there's a 50 percent chance of passing it on to my children. And pregnancy could accelerate my vision loss. Then I think about the fact that I may never see what my children look like. But I'll get to touch them and smell them—I think I'll know my children in a different way.

My doctors say it's possible that I will completely lose my hearing and vision in just a few years. It's finally becoming believable. But I think I'm ready to deal with it. I'll soon be a candidate for a cochlear implant, which will require major surgery but could drastically improve my hearing. If all goes well, I'll never live in total silence. But one of these days, I'll actually start using that cane. I try to stay optimistic. At 19, I couldn't imagine I'd have as much loss as I do now. But I'm OK. It's my life, and I don't have time for fear.

Hearing Loss Creeps Up on a Naval Officer

Chris Plummer

A noisy environment can lead to hearing loss—even when a person wears ear protection. That is the hard lesson naval officer Chris Plummer learned, as he relates in the following viewpoint. As a young man just out of flight school, he began to wear double protection for his ears on the flight deck of his aircraft carrier. Looking back, however, Plummer realizes that the noise hazards were not confined to the deck alone. Ear-shattering levels of noise were everywhere on the craft, including his bunk. Even as he slept, the catapult that launches planes off the deck of the carrier over his head was damaging the delicate hairs and nerves that turn sounds into hearing. On shore, he began to recognize that life at sea was very noisy, and eventually he began to realize that he was losing his hearing, but it was too late to prevent the loss. Today, he uses protection in every hazardous situation, but he has already lost an irretrievable portion of his senses. Plummer flew fighter planes off the deck of an aircraft carrier, accumulating five thousand hours of flight time. He is stationed at the office of the chief of naval operations in Washington, D.C.

SOURCE: Chris Plummer, "Are You Deaf?" *Sea & Shore,* Winter 2008–09, pp. 18–19.

"Are you deaf?" That's what my wife jokingly used to ask me anytime I watched TV or listened to the stereo. I'd reply, "No, I just like stuff louder."

The jokes about my minor physical disability stopped, though, when the flight surgeons readjusted my baseline for an annual hearing test. I had become good at the standard tricks for passing the test but realized the only person I was fooling was myself. Now I'm working hard to conserve the hearing I have left after many years as a naval aviator aboard aircraft carriers where loud noise is a recognized occupational hazard.

You couldn't tell I had a problem to look at me, but the junior officers and Sailors in my squadron always knew it when they talked to me. My wife and kids knew it, too, when I watched a blaring TV. More importantly, I knew it every year when I stepped into an audiology booth for my annual flight physical. My hearing was lousy, and it hadn't been that way when I joined the Navy. The loss had been a slow, almost imperceptible process—one that didn't have to happen.

Extra Protection

After flight school, I always wore double-hearing protection in the cockpit—a combination of those little yellow foamies you wad up and stick in your ears and a flight helmet. Aboard an aircraft carrier, though, it's not enough just to wear hearing protection while flying airplanes off the flight deck. Any cruise veteran will tell you how painfully deafening it is to be caught unaware on the 03 level under the arresting gear while an aircraft lands or under a catapult when an aircraft goes to full power. The ship abounds with incessant and traumatic assaults on your ears, and it's not only during flight operations.

I'm convinced the noise level from daily maintenance in some areas of the ship is harmful. Here is my common-sense approach: If it hurts your ears, it's too loud. There also are lots of background noises. Even the ship's ventilation system produces an annoying hum. You get so used to these noises, though, that you stop hearing them.

A Boom-Box Revelation

I'll never forget returning home from my first cruise and finding my boom-box as I unpacked. I plugged it in and cranked the volume to my standard "cruise" setting, which turned out to be earsplitting. At that point, I realized how loud life is aboard ship.

My ears always hurt when I was on the flight deck with my hearing protection on, and as a Tomcat went into afterburner on the catapult. That was a good thing, though; it meant I still could hear. I wore earplugs at night when I hit the rack and when flight ops were going on. Sleeping directly below a catapult, I knew if the noise was painful when I was awake, it also would damage my ears when I was asleep. I stopped waiting to climb into the cockpit before putting on double-hearing protection. I put it on before stepping onto the flight deck and walking to my aircraft.

When on the flight deck for FOD [foreign object debris] walkdown, a jog, or just to check on the maintenance when flight ops were secured, I had a pair of foamies with me. There are a thousand ear-piercing noisemakers on the flight deck and all over a ship just waiting to get you when you're least prepared. You never know when a helicopter is going to arrive on the roof, or a huffer is going to turn in the hangar bay. As an extra precaution, I even started taking a pair of foamies to the gym. . . .

> **FAST FACT**
>
> Combat is a major threat to hearing for military personnel. Soldiers sent to battle zones are over fifty times more likely to suffer noise-induced hearing loss than are those who do not deploy.

Too Late to Recover

I started taking precautions at home, too. I became perhaps the biggest nerd in my neighborhood. If I mowed the lawn, I wore hearing protection. If I used a power tool, like a drill, I wore hearing and eye protection. I took no

The author believes that the cacophony of noises produced by daily flight operations aboard a U.S. Navy aircraft carrier caused his gradual hearing loss. (**AP Images**)

chances and operated in a max-conserve mode. When I was around my kids, I turned down the stereo because I didn't want to pass on my problem to the next generation. None of these things could help me regain any of my hearing loss, but they helped me hold on to what I have left.

It's really too bad you can't take a picture of hearing loss. There are some real eye-grabbing photos for people who smoke, chew tobacco, or don't wear eye protection. Nearly everyone in the fleet has seen the poster of the poor fellow whose ring degloved his finger. I removed my wedding band the very day I first saw that gruesome image and haven't worn it since. If there had been an eye-arresting Kodak moment to depict the misfortune of hearing loss, I perhaps would have been more cautious.

I miss hearing all the high notes of a violin concerto, and it annoys me that telephones don't ring very loud any more. It's also a nuisance to constantly lean forward and cup my ears during a normal conversation. Take heed young Sailors; become believers right now, and leave the Navy with the same ears you entered it with. I wish I could.

Like Father, Like Daughter— or Maybe Not

Patty Therre

Of all disabilities, deafness has one of the most profound effects on family members. In the following viewpoint Patty Therre unfolds a remarkable story. Her father lost his hearing suddenly and mysteriously when he was a young adult. His reaction was to try to hide his disability, and his wife and children became his only means to communicate with the world. After the death of her mother, Therre found herself thrown back into the role of interpreter for an increasingly dependent father. Then, quite suddenly, she began to lose her hearing, too. The struggle to come to terms with this double dose of fate forms the climax of her story. Therre is an online writer and publisher specializing in consumer and beauty products.

"**A**m I going to be deaf like my father?" I asked the short, balding ear specialist who was seeing me for the third time in a month for a serious ear infection. I was nine years old at the time and clutching tightly to my mother's hand, terrified of the answer.

SOURCE: Patty Therre, "I Am Going Deaf Like My Father—Or Am I? My Story . . . ," Epinions.com, January 19, 2005. Reproduced by permission of the author.

"No, you don't have the same type of ear problem as your father. You'll be fine," he said and smiled reassuringly.

I let out a sigh of relief. My father lost his hearing at age twenty-one. I never knew him as a hearing person; I was born long after his hearing was gone.

Fearing Father's Fate

No one knew why my father lost his hearing and no one could restore it. Hearing aids were useless. He was left in silence, a silence that, even at age nine, I was terrified I would somehow be plunged into. I was the only one of my four siblings who suffered from ear infections and the only one who spent more time at the Ear, Nose and Throat specialist than at school. But, I was assured, I didn't have my father's type of problem. His was sensory (nerve) deafness. My problem was middle ear infections. Vastly different situations which, I was told, should alleviate any fears I may have about my hearing. Even at nine years old, I was skeptical. My father and I were so much alike in many ways that it seemed almost inevitable to me that I would end up like him someday.

My father is a fiercely stubborn man and, even now at 79 years old, he refuses to read lips or allow anyone to use any type of sign language. We developed a special way of talking to him that only the immediate family knew. It was a secret language all our own. I had no idea growing up that my father spent his entire adult life completely isolated from the outside world. It was as natural to me to write in the air and use our code to talk to him as it was for others to simply speak to their fathers.

Ear Infections Subside

As I grew older, my ear infections lessened and eventually only hounded me a couple times a year. I would get antibiotics and be as good as new after a few days. Still, I always had a nagging thought in my mind. Since we didn't know why my father went deaf, how could anyone truly reassure me that I wouldn't? But the answer was the same whenever I asked. "You don't have the type of ear problem your father does. Relax and don't worry."

For years, I didn't worry. I was busy getting married, having babies and editing a major professional wrestling magazine. Life was good. I was no longer worried about my hearing and ear infections were a rarity.

When my mother suffered a brain aneurysm in 1992 and complications caused her to remain in the hospital for four long years and my youngest son became seriously ill at the same time, my own health and well-being was the furthest thing from my mind. Handling Mom's day-to-day decision making with the doctors, traveling out of state for health care for my son, and being there for my dad came first.

Father Needs Care

When my mother died in 1996, my son was no longer ill, and I felt a guilty rush of relief to be finally without the suffering around me that haunted me day and night for years.

I was completely unaware that my father was so isolated until after my mother's death. She was his translator, his ticket to the outside world. When she passed away, he was completely alone with no ability to communicate with anyone outside of the family. He could and can speak fine, but he couldn't understand anything anyone said to him. He was lost and alone in the world.

Taking care of my father is amazingly strenuous. He is no longer able to understand my sisters so I have the bulk of responsibility of explaining everything to him from what his health ailments are to what is happening in the family. I leave his nursing home with a sense of grief for him, sitting in silence, completely cut off from

> **FAST FACT**
>
> According to the American Hearing Research Foundation, sudden hearing loss occurs in up to 20 people per 100,000 and accounts for 1 percent of all sensorineural hearing loss cases.

the rest of the world, not in the hearing world yet not truly in the deaf world.

Recently, I noticed that I was having trouble hearing the television at times and missing words here and there when people talked to me. I hadn't been to an ear specialist in years but decided to get a hearing test to be sure all was well. It wasn't.

Trouble Begins

After several tests and procedures, I was told that I have profound hearing loss in the high frequency range and mild to moderate hearing loss in the moderate range. I tried steroids, tubes in my ears and allergy medications, all to no avail.

At last, I sat down with the same doctor whom I saw thirty years ago. He is semi-retired now but sees "difficult" patients of which I am one. He explained to me that I was losing my hearing. It could be gradual or it could come suddenly. Hearing aids generally are of very little help for my type of hearing loss. When my hearing is nearly completely gone, I may be a candidate for a cochlear implant, which is a tiny receptor implanted in the ear to help boost sounds and give a deaf person some hope of hearing, albeit not like a typical hearing person would.

I grimly listened to the doctor explain all this to me and then I asked, "So, I am going deaf like my father?" This time, the answer was "Yes."

We don't know why my father lost his hearing and we don't know why I am. It has nothing to do with my previous ear infections as my hearing loss is sensory which is in the inner ear and the infections cause damage to the middle ear. At 40, I know that soon, I will be deaf.

When I left the doctor's office, I was stunned. I honestly never expected to be told that I truly was losing my hearing and that nothing at all could stop or even slow down the progression. After the news sank in, I felt terrified.

Deafness Looms

I thought of my father, sitting in his little room in a nursing home where he doesn't belong, all alone. I thought of the way people throughout the years screamed at him, thinking somehow he would hear them if they shouted, despite the fact he couldn't hear anything no matter how loud it was. I thought of all the things in life that he missed—the sound of his children's first cries, our first words, the birds on a bright sunny day, music. He has not heard music since 1946. The thought of him missing all those eras of beautiful music alone wounds me.

When I see my father, I see a man who refused to acknowledge his hearing loss and who wanted no part of the deaf world. Sign language, to him, was too theatrical and would draw unwanted attention. Lip reading was something he could never grasp and was too embarrassed to take lessons to help him learn. He spent the major part of his life bluffing his way through conversations by nodding and acting as though he had some idea what people were saying but really have none at all. My mother was his saving grace. Her ability to clue him in to what was happening around him without drawing attention was astounding. Later, my sisters and brother and I would learn to do the same thing.

Still, he missed out on so much of life by staying at home, away from situations where he would potentially be embarrassed by his deafness, and resorting to alcohol to soothe his pain. His life essentially was over and he just existed after his hearing loss.

Not Like Her Father

The day I was told that I was going to end up deaf "like my father" was the day I decided that I needed to be proactive and embrace the future, not run from it. I ordered several sign language books and have begun teaching myself sign. I am taking a six video course on lip reading (also called speech reading) and am doing fairly well, although it is so frustrating to see people's lips move yet not hear what they are saying, but I know that will be my fate and I want to be prepared. I have discussed late onset hearing loss with those who have already experienced it and I have started to think of myself more as a hard of hearing person rather than a hearing person.

The day I joined an online community called "Deafies" was the day I knew that I would not follow in my father's footsteps. Yes, I will lose the ability to hear music, to hear my sons talk to me, and to enjoy a movie with sound, but I will not isolate myself from the world and I refuse to be embarrassed about my hearing loss and impending deafness.

I was taught from the day I was born that being deaf is looked upon by most people as being stupid. I was taught to hide the fact that my father couldn't hear and to secretly code words to him so that he seemed to be understanding what people were saying. I was taught that deafness was something to be ashamed of. Despite forty years of hiding and covering up for my father's deafness—or maybe because of it—I refuse to hide mine. I have told everyone I know what is going to happen and I have prepared myself to be deeply saddened and to grieve for the loss of one of my most important senses.

Casting Shame Aside

But I will not feel shame because I cannot hear. I will not sit in the corner and shy away from people because of my hearing loss and I will never put my children through the rituals I went through with my father. I will stand tall. I will accept my fate. I will have the tools I need to get by in the hearing world despite the fact that I will no longer be in that world.

When the day comes—and I can tell that it won't be years, but months—I will give myself permission to cry and to crawl into bed and pull the covers over my head and stay there for a week.

Then I will get on with my life the best way I can. I will have already learned sign language and will have my lip reading course to continue practicing as often as possible.

I plan to meet very soon with a representative from AURORA, a resource agency for the deaf and blind, to order several items I need: a TTY [teletypewriter], machine for communicating by phone, a doorbell flasher, smoke alarm flasher, a bed shaker to wake me up for morning appointments, and whatever else they have to make my transition from hearing into silence easier. I hope to have these items in place by the time my hearing is gone.

None of these things will make the loss of my hearing easier to bear but they will make my life less isolated. I watched what isolation and dependency does to a deaf person for 40 years and I don't want that same fate.

Dad in Denial

My father refuses to believe that this is happening to me. Once again, he is in denial. I don't force the issue; he doesn't need to know too much about what I am going through right now. He had his own hell, he doesn't need to be a part of mine. Still, now and then when he

As she gradually loses her hearing the author is busy gathering items like a teletypewriter, with which she will be able to use a telephone, various alarm flashers, and a bed shaker to wake her up.
(Doug Martin/Photo Researchers, Inc.)

is in a rare open mood, he shares stories with me of the name-calling that happened when he was young and of the desperation he felt when he realized his hearing was truly gone. I listen intently to his stories, wanting to weep at the cruelty inflicted on him by his family, friends and strangers. I want to go back in time and change things so that he could better cope when he lost his hearing. I can't go back in time but I can do one thing for my father even though he may not realize I am doing it.

I can continue his legacy of courage and strength and, with it, I can make a statement to the world that deaf people are not stupid and they are not ashamed. This, I will do for my father who endured years of suffering because of his refusal to accept his disability.

I am going to be the deaf person my father always wanted to be but didn't have the strength or resources to be. I will make my dad proud by not living the same type of life he did.

The answer to my question "Am I going deaf like my father?" is really no, I am not. I am going deaf. But not like my father. And I intend to make as many people as I can aware of the fact that there is life after hearing loss, not just existence.

GLOSSARY

acquired deafness   A loss of hearing that develops after birth.

American Sign Language (ASL)   A manual sign language used mainly by the deaf in North America.

audiologist   A professional trained in the science of hearing who specializes in assessment and rehabilitation of people with hearing disorders.

auditory canal   The structure that leads from the outer ear to the eardrum (tympanic membrane).

cochlea   Snail-shaped structure in the inner ear containing the organ of hearing.

cochlear implant   A surgically implanted electronic device that replaces a defective cochlea and turns sounds into electrical impulses fed into the hearing path in the brain.

CODA   An acronym for "Children of Deaf Adults," usually applied to hearing children.

conductive hearing loss   Hearing loss that results from a blockage or malfunction of the outer or middle ear.

congenital deafness   Deafness present at birth.

deaf   A term describing a severe to total inability to hear. When written with a capital "D," it connotes Deaf culture.

Deaf culture   Denoted by a capital "D," it is the culture developed by deaf people whose native language is American Sign Language and who embrace their condition as a positive attribute to be shared with others of similar outlook.

decibel (dB)	A unit of measurement used in determining the intensity of sounds.
fingerspelling	A portion of a manual language in which the letters in an alphabet, and sometimes numerals, are conveyed using only the hands.
hard of hearing	Descriptor of a person with significant hearing loss who is still able to function in the hearing world, possibly with hearing aids.
hearing aid	Any of various devices that receive, amplify, and sometimes filter sounds and then transmit them into the ear of the wearer.
hearing impaired	A term that may denote someone with partial hearing loss or may cover the range of people from partial hearing to entirely deaf. The term is controversial among those in the Deaf community who reject the idea of deafness as a disability.
lipreading	Also known as speech reading, it is the skill of interpreting language from a person's lip movements without being able to hear the sounds of speech.
manual language	*See* sign language.
oral deaf	A prelingually deaf person who relies on oral communication rather than sign language.
oralism	A philosophy and method of deaf education that relies on teaching lipreading and speech production to the exclusion of any sign language.
postlingually deaf	A person who became deaf after acquiring a spoken language.
prelingually deaf	A person who became deaf prior to acquiring a spoken language.
sign language	A manual language that uses a system of hand gestures, facial gestures, and other body movements as the means of communication, especially among deaf people.

tinnitus | Medical term for the false perception of sound (often referred to as "ringing in the ears"). The perceived hissing, roaring, whistling, chirping, or clicking interferes with the hearing of actual sounds.

Usher syndrome | A hereditary disease that degrades hearing, vision, and sometimes balance.

CHRONOLOGY

B.C.   ca. 1000   The Hebrew Talmud offers some protections to the deaf but excludes them from bearing witness in trials or fully participating in religious rituals.

440   The ancient Greek writer Herodotus notes that one of the sons of King Croesus was deaf.

355   The Greek philosopher Aristotle pronounces those born deaf incapable of reasoning or learning.

A.D.   ca. 1550   First known instances of deaf education begin with mathematician Gerolamo Cardano of Padua, Italy, who attempts to teach his deaf son using written symbols.

1620   The Spanish priest Juan Pablo Bonet publishes the first manual alphabet.

1754   French priest Abbé Charles Michel de l'Épée founds the first school in France for the deaf. He also creates an enduring French sign language.

ca. 1790   The hearing trumpet, a conical device inserted in the ear, helps the hearing impaired.

1817   In Connecticut, Thomas Hopkins Gallaudet and others found the Hartford Asylum for the Education and Instruction of the Deaf and Dumb, which later becomes known as the American School for the Deaf.

1846   The journal *American Annals of the Deaf* begins publication at the American School for the Deaf in Hartford, Connecticut.

1864   President Abraham Lincoln signs legislation giving the Columbia Institution for the Deaf (later renamed Gallaudet University) the authority to confer college degrees, making it the first college expressly for the deaf.

1872   Inventor Alexander Graham Bell opens a school for hearing and hearing-impaired children. It emphasizes oral education only.

1880   The National Association of the Deaf is founded.

1898   The Akouphone Company manufactures the first electrical hearing aid. Expensive and clumsy, it fails to catch on.

1925   The Siemens Company produces a hearing aid with an electronic amplifier built in.

1957   French doctor André Djourno performs the first cochlear implant surgery.

1975   President Gerald Ford signs a bill guaranteeing disabled children the right to a free, appropriate education.

1985   The United States approves cochlear implant trials.

1986   Marlee Matlin, a deaf actress, wins an Oscar in her debut film performance.

1987   The digital hearing aid is invented.

1992 President George H.W. Bush signs the Americans with Disabilities Act.

1995 Heather Whitestone, an orally educated deaf woman from Birmingham, Alabama, is crowned Miss America.

2008 Genetic researchers independently make discoveries that give hope of an eventual gene therapy cure for deafness.

ORGANIZATIONS TO CONTACT

The editors have compiled the following list of organizations concerned with the issues debated in this book. The descriptions are derived from materials provided by the organizations. All have publications or information available for interested readers. The list was compiled on the date of publication of the present volume; the information provided here may change. Be aware that many organizations take several weeks or longer to respond to inquiries, so allow as much time as possible.

Alexander Graham Bell Association for the Deaf and Hard of Hearing
3417 Volta Pl. NW
Washington, DC 20007
(202) 337-5220
TTY: (202) 337-5221
fax: (202) 337-8314
www.agbell.org

The Alexander Graham Bell Association for the Deaf and Hard of Hearing helps families, health-care providers, and education professionals understand childhood hearing loss and the importance of early diagnosis and intervention. In keeping with the philosophy of its founder, Alexander Graham Bell, inventor of the telephone, it supports oral communication for the deaf through advocacy, education, research, and financial aid.

American Society for Deaf Children (ASDC)
3820 Hartzdale Dr.
Camp Hill, PA 17011
(866) 895-4206
fax: (717) 909-5599
www.deafchildren.org

The American Society for Deaf Children was founded in 1967 to support and educate families of deaf children and advocate on their behalf. It offers a Parent-to-Parent Network to aid new parents of deaf children and a Parents Connected Network for keeping up with legislative issues, among other services. It also publishes *Endeavor* magazine, aimed at providing useful information to families with deaf children.

Deaf and Hard of Hearing Alliance (DHHA)
444 North Capitol St. NW, Ste. 601
Washington, DC 20001
(202) 347-0034
fax: (202) 347-0037
www.dhhainfo.com

The Deaf and Hard of Hearing Alliance is a coalition of civic and professional organizations that represent people with hearing loss. It formed to influence federal public policy that can improve the quality of life for people who are deaf or hard of hearing. The DHHA allows organizations that disagree on some issues to come together to advocate for the interests of the deaf and hard of hearing community in areas of consensus.

Deafness Research Foundation (DRF)
641 Lexington Ave., 5th Floor
New York, NY 10022-4503
(212) 328-9480 or
(866) 454-3924
TTY: (888) 435-6104
fax: (212) 328-9484
www.drf.org

The Deafness Research Foundation is the leading national source of private funding for basic and clinical research in hearing science. Its mission is to make possible a lifetime of healthy hearing and balance through quality research, education, and advocacy. Since its founding in 1958, DRF has awarded over twenty-two hundred grants, totaling over $24 million. Grants have promoted the development of cochlear implants, hair cell regeneration, and universal newborn hearing sceening, among other developments.

Hearing Loss Association of America (HLAA)
7910 Woodmont Ave., Ste. 1200
Bethesda, MD 20814
(301) 657-2248
fax: (301) 913-9413
www.hearingloss.org

The Hearing Loss Association of America is the nation's leading organization representing people with hearing loss. The HLAA provides assistance and resources for people with hearing loss and their families to learn how to adjust to living with hearing loss. It works to eradicate the stigma associated with hearing loss and to raise public awareness about the need for prevention and for regular hearing screenings throughout life.

Laurent Clerc National Deaf Education Center
800 Florida Ave. NE
Washington, DC
20002-3695
(202) 651-5855
(Voice/TTY)
clerc.center@gallaudet
.edu

The Laurent Clerc National Deaf Education Center at Gallaudet University provides information, training, and technical assistance for parents and professionals to meet the needs of children who are deaf or hard of hearing. Its mission is to improve the quality of education afforded to deaf and hard of hearing students from birth to age twenty-one throughout the United States.

National Association of the Deaf (NAD)
8630 Fenton St., Ste. 820
Silver Spring, MD 20910
(301) 587-1788
TTY: (301) 587-1789
fax: (301) 587-1791
www.nad.org

The National Association of the Deaf is the nation's oldest civil rights organization representing deaf and hard of hearing people in the United States. Established in 1880, the NAD was shaped by deaf leaders who believed in the right of the American deaf community to use sign language, to congregate on issues important to them, and to have its interests represented at the national level. These beliefs remain true to the present, with the right to learn and use American Sign Language as a core value.

National Black Deaf Advocates
6774 Cobble Creek Rd., Apt. 2C
Whitsett, NC 27377
www.nbda.org

National Black Deaf Advocates exists to promote leadership development, economic and educational opportunities, social equality, and to safeguard the general health and welfare of black deaf and hard of hearing people. Founded in 1982, it serves African American adults who are deaf or hard of hearing; parents of African American children who are deaf or hard of hearing; and professionals who work with deaf and hard of hearing children and adults, people of color, and other interested individuals.

Telecommunications for the Deaf and Hard of Hearing, Inc. (TDI)
8630 Fenton St., #604
Silver Spring, MD 20910
(301) 589-3786
TTY: (301) 589-3006
fax: (301) 589-3797
www.tdi-online.org

TDI was established in 1968 originally to promote further distribution of teletypewriters (TTYs) in the deaf community and to publish an annual national directory of TTY numbers. It currently serves as a national advocacy organization focusing its energies and resources on addressing equal access issues in telecommunications, media, and information technologies for people who are deaf, hard of hearing, late-deafened, or deaf-blind.

World Federation of the Deaf (WFD)
PO Box 65, FIN-00401
Helsinki, FINLAND
fax: +358 9 580 3572
www.wfdeaf.org

The World Federation of the Deaf began in 1951 at a world congress of the deaf. Its membership from 130 countries represents 70 million deaf people around the globe. WFD supports and promotes in its work the many United Nations conventions on human rights, with a focus on deaf people who use sign language, and their friends and family.

FOR FURTHER READING

Books

Sally Austen and Susan Crocker, *Deafness in Mind*. Hoboken, NJ: John Wiley & Sons, 2004.

Leah Hagar Cohen, *Train Go Sorry: Inside a Deaf World*. Boston: Houghton Mifflin, 1994.

Bainy Cyrus, Eileen Katz, and Frances M. Parsons, *Deaf Women's Lives: Three Self-Portraits*. Washington, DC: Gallaudet University Press, 2005.

ICON Health, *Hearing Impairment: A Medical Dictionary, Bibliography, and Annotated Research Guide to Internet References*. San Diego: ICON Health, 2004.

Harlan Lane, *When the Mind Hears: A History of the Deaf*. New York: Random House, 1989.

Marc Marschark and Patricia Elizabeth Spencer, eds., *Oxford Handbook of Deaf Studies, Language, and Education*. New York: Oxford University Press, 2003.

Richard Medugno, *Deaf Daughter, Hearing Father*. Washington, DC: Gallaudet University Press, 2005.

Ruth A. Morgan-Jones, *Hearing Differently: The Impact of Hearing Impairment on Family Life*. Hoboken, NJ: John Wiley & Sons, 2001.

Carol Padden and Tom Humphries, *Inside Deaf Culture*. Cambridge, MA: Harvard University Press, 2005.

Martha A. Sheridan, *Deaf Adolescents: Inner Lives and Lifeworld Development*. Washington, DC: Gallaudet University Press, 2008.

Periodicals and Internet Sources

Neil Bauman, "The Bizarre World of Extreme Reverse-Slope (or Low Frequency) Hearing Loss," Center for Hearing Loss Help, April 2007. www.hearinglosshelp.com/articles/reverseslopelong.htm.

David Brand, "This Is the Selma of the Deaf," *Time*, June 24, 2001.

Susan Brink, "A Deaf Couple's Late-Life Cochlear Implant," *Los Angeles Times*, May 6, 2008.

Henri E. Cauvin and Steve Hendrix, "D.C. Stadium Ordered to Address Needs of Deaf Fans," *Washington Post*, October 3, 2008.

Shi Davidi, "Mariners Prospect Tyson Gillies Turns Negative of Hearing Loss into Positive," *Canadian Press*, July 20, 2009.

Jane K. Fernandes, "Many Ways of Being Deaf," *Washington Post*, October 14, 2006.

Samuel G. Freedman, "Nearly Deaf Professor Teaches English Literacy, One Student at a Time," *New York Times*, May 21, 2008.

Steve Friess, "Subtitles: Deaf to the Problem," *Newsweek*, February 27, 2006.

Thomas Goldsmith, "Researchers Work to Refine Cochlear Implants," *Raleigh News & Observer*, June 9, 2009.

Aaron Gould, "Deaf Comic Gets Rave Reviews from Both Hearing and Hearing Impaired," *Olympic College Olympian*, January 27, 2009.

HealthDay, "Deaf Children Can Create Own Sign Language," February 17, 2009. http://health.usnews.com/articles/health/healthday/2009/02/17/deaf-children-can-create-own-sign-language.html.

John Horgan, "A Sign Is Born: Language Unfolds Among Deaf Nicaraguan Children," *Scientific American*, December 1995.

Medical News Today, "The Not-So-Silent Crisis: 49% of North Americans Put Their Hearing at Risk Every Week, Yet Majority Go Untested for Years," May 7, 2009. www.medicalnewstoday.com/articles/149262.php.

Donald F. Moores, "Residential Schools for the Deaf and Academic Placement Past, Present, and Future," editorial, *American Annals of the Deaf*, Spring 2009.

Karen Plumley, "Working with Deaf and Hard of Hearing Students: Interpreters, American Sign Language, and Teachers of the Deaf," *Suite 101*, January 26, 2009. http://deaf-students .suite101.com/article.cfm/working_with_the_deaf_and_hard_ of_hearing.

Mark Pratt, "Researchers Developing Sign Language Dictionary," Associated Press, May 25, 2008.

Julie Salomon, "Driven to Help the Hard of Hearing," *New York Times*, April 5, 2005.

Lloyd de Vries, "MP3s May Threaten Hearing Loss," CBS News, August 25, 2005. www.cbsnews.com.

DeWayne Wickham, "Deaf Golfer's Drive for Life Is a Story Worth Hearing," *USA Today*, January 22, 2008.

Timothy Wilson, "Faster Phones for the Deaf," *Washington Post*, December 4, 2008.

Gregg Zoroya, "Soldier's Story Illustrates Risks of Hearing Loss in War," *USA Today*, August 4, 2008.

INDEX

A

Age-related hearing loss, 17–18, 22, 23
Alexander, Rebecca, 109–114
American Sign Language (ASL)
  Deaf culture and, 61–62, 78–79, 92
  development of, 12
  as natural language, 82–83
  teaching of, 104–105
Audiologists, 51–52
Audism, 68, 77
Auditory system, problems in,
  24–29
Auditory-verbal therapy, 90

B

Baker, Virginia, 58
Balance
  hearing loss and, 24–29
  inner ear and, 26
Beck, Dan, 36, 37
Beethoven, Ludwig van, 9
Behind-the-ear aids, 48–49
Bell, Alexander Graham, 12
Benedict, Dwight, 81
Benign Paroxysmal Positional Vertigo
  (BPPV), 28–29
Big Honcho Media, 37
Branson, Richard, 36

C

Casterline, Dorothy, 61
Central auditory processing disorders,
  18–19

Chasin, Marshall, 32
Childhood deafness, 21
Children
  deaf, 79–80, 83–84, 93
  with deaf parents, 101–108,
    119–126
  ear infections in, 27, 28
Chloesteatoma, 27
Civil rights legislation, 12–13
Clerc, Laurent, 11
Closed captioning, 13
Cochlea, 17–18, 56
Cochlear implants
  benefits of, 53–58, 85–88
  controversy over, 13–14, 75
  effectiveness of, 80, 81
  hybrid, 55–58
  indicators for, 41–43
  for presbycusis, 22
  quality of sound provided by, 23
  risks of, 86, 89–93
Cochlear otosclerosis, 99
Columbia Institute for the Deaf, 12,
  13, 80
Common sense, 9
Conductive hearing loss, 18, 22
Congenital hearing loss, 19–20
  causes of, 39–45
  newborn screening for, 38–45
Connexin 26 mutations, 40, 41
Croneberg, Carl, 61
Cytomegalovirus (CMV), 39,
  44–45